Agile Project Management with Scrum

Secret Scrum Formulas and Methods in Agile Project Management.

© Copyright 2019 - All rights reserved. Alex Campbell.

The content contained within this book may not be reproduced, duplicated or transmitted without direct written permission from the author or the publisher.

Under no circumstances will any blame or legal responsibility be held against the publisher, or author, for any damages, reparation, or monetary loss due to the information contained within this book. Either directly or indirectly.

Legal Notice:
This book is copyright protected. This book is only for personal use. You cannot amend, distribute, sell, use, quote or paraphrase any part, or the content within this book, without the consent of the author or publisher.

Disclaimer Notice:
Please note the information contained within this document is for educational and entertainment purposes only. All effort has been executed to present accurate, up to date, and reliable, complete information. No warranties of any kind are declared or implied. Readers acknowledge that the author is not engaging in the rendering of legal, financial, medical or professional advice. The content within this book has been derived from various sources. Please consult a licensed professional before attempting any techniques outlined in this book.

By reading this document, the reader agrees that under no circumstances is the author responsible for any losses, direct or indirect, which are incurred as a result of the use of information contained within this document, including, but not limited to, — errors, omissions, or inaccuracies.

TABLE OF CONTENTS

Introduction 1

Chapter One: The Basics – Recap of the Main Concepts 5
    How Project Management Is Categorized 5
    What Is Agile Project Management? 9
    What Is Scrum? 11
    What Does a Scrum Roadmap Look Like? 13

Chapter Two: Putting Agile Scrum in Relation to Traditional Project Management 18
    The End of the Project 18
    Incomplete Tasks 19
    Schedule, Budget, Quality 20
    Time Management 20
    Communication 22
    Handling Requirements 23
    The Depth of the Work Breakdown Structure 24
    Control and Command Over the Project 25
    Quality Issues 26
    Risk Management 27
    Feedback Loops 29
    Dependencies 30

Chapter Three: Scrum and the Waterfall Method 32
    Scrum and Waterfall? 35
    How to Implement Scrum in Skeptical Teams 37
    Bringing Together the Waterfall Method and the Scrum Method 38

Chapter Four: Implementing Scrum Management as a Line Manager 44

Chapter Five: Scrum Problem Solving Techniques 48
    1. Scrum vs. Six Sigma: The Perfect Couple 48
    2. Scrum vs. The Eight Disciplines: The Close Siblings 55
    3. Scrum vs. The 5 Whys: The Friendly Neighbors....................... 58

Chapter Six: The Multiple and Varied Uses of Scrum 62
    Scrum in the Educational System 62
    Scrum and the Service Industry 65
    Scrum and the Health Industry 66

Chapter Seven: Bring Your Scrum to the Next Level with Soft Skills and the Right Mindset 68
    Create a Good Ambiance 71

Chapter Eight: The Skills of a Great Scrum Master 80
    Mastery of Scrum Beyond the Rules.. 81

Chapter Nine: The Shining Skills of a Scrum Team 88
    Going for the Jedi, Guru, Rockstar and Ninja................................. 89
    Adherence to Scrum Values... 90

Chapter Ten: Implementing Scrum with your Team 93
    The Meaningful Metrics to Mind 93
    The Best Characteristics of a Successful Standup......................... 96
    Drawing an Adequate Task Board... 99

Conclusion 100

Bibliography 105

Introduction

There used to be a joke saying that there are two types of project managers: those who forward emails to the assigned team members and those who rephrase those emails.

In reality, however, project management is far less simplistic than that; it is the kind of knowledge that lies at the confluence between science and art, between philosophy and methodology, between the Old and the New.

To someone working outside of the project management spectrum, this entire sphere might seem very simple and straightforward: you take a project, analyze its risks and opportunities, split it in various tasks, make sure your team follows through with the work on these tasks, and then plain and simply deliver it.

True, if we were to undress project management to its very basics, that's what it is.

To compare this with cars, the very basic, naked elements of project management are somewhat the same with the main functionality of a car and the way it works: an engine fuels movement based on a specific type of fuel, and that movement pushes the wheels further in the direction you are steering the wheel.

However, anyone who drives a car knows that there are multiple other factors that influence whether or not that car is good. You will get from point A to point B in any car you might drive, but the way you do this, and the safety involved in the entire process will be considerably different.

Imagine driving 500 miles in a Tesla manufactured in 2019 and driving the same distance in a 1970s Ford that has been running ever since and has crossed the distance between the Earth and the Moon a few hundreds of times. Not only will you be more comfortable in the first car, but you will also be safer, will have more certainty that the car will take you to point B without breaking, and you will do it in a lesser amount of time.

The same goes with project management as well. At its very core, it's all about making sure a team is working on its tasks and that those tasks will eventually come together for the final deliverable.

In practice, however, project management can take almost as many facets and forms as car manufacturers and technologies in the world. And it is precisely in those variations that you will find true value.

There are a few project management methodologies used at the moment. Some are very popular and others are less popular, but what brings them all together is the fact that they all focus on *delivering a good product, on time, within the budget,* the same way a car's system focuses on igniting the engine to allow you to steer the wheels in your preferred direction.

Scrum project management is only but a small slice of the project management cake. As I was showing in a previous book about beginner techniques to use with Scrum Project Management, the very basics of this approach are quite easy to understand once you fully comprehend the scope and the advantages this specific approach brings to the table.

In order to apply Scrum project management and reap all the benefits it has to offer, you must fully understand where it lies in comparison with other project management methods, whether they are traditional or not.

Knowing this will allow you respond better to a variety of situations where Scrum may either come as a complement, or it may require an overlay created from some of the concepts common in other project management methods.

Why can't you simply stick to Scrum once and for all?

Because project management deals not in terms of certainties and planning, but in terms of uncertainties. Project management is, beyond all methodologies and rules and spreadsheets and charts, an activity that handles *humans*.

And if there's something on this Earth more complex than the explanation of how the Universe will end, that is most certainly the *human being itself*.

As a project manager, you will have to deal with humans, your team members, all with their own personalities and sets of expertise, your superiors, other companies, other teams, and so on. If everyone in the world only knew Scrum, you could easily lay back and simply use this fun and efficient approach forever and ever.

But the world doesn't use Scrum only, and in all honesty, it shouldn't do so, because no matter how much I love this method, it is not always the best of choices, in certain circumstances. Even more, some people completely refuse to use Scrum, either because it is in the human nature to be suspicious of the "new element" or because it simply doesn't fit their particular situation.

So, in order to step up your Scrum game and implement techniques that pertain to a more advanced level, you have to comprehend the relationship between Scrum and other popular project management methods, as well as how they all connect to each other when necessary.

The first part of this book will be dedicated entirely to that: providing you with the information and examples that will help you put Scrum project management in perspective.

The second part of this book will be dedicated to another very important parallel in building your Scrum expertise: the human factor.

Working with human beings as a project manager is not only about their resilience when faced with something new and their adversity when facing change. It is also about building teams of people who actually value your input and guidance.

It is about inspiring those people the same way the martial arts master inspires his/ her students to work harder, be better, do more, be more humble, and so on.

Soft skills are essential regardless of what your chosen project management method may be. But when it comes to Scrum, these apparently insignificant skills will make all the difference in the world. Together with the right mindset they will help you build the kind of Scrum team that proves beyond all reasonable doubt that this method is legit, that it works, and that it can yield truly fantastic results.

This book is all about liaison.

The liaison between Scrum and other project management frameworks and methodologies, as well as the liaison between you and your team members and the liaison between your team members and the core values of Scrum as a work ethic and even as a life philosophy.

I invite you on a journey of pushing the boundaries and expanding the knowledge. Hopefully, by the end of this, you will have gained a much better understanding of Scrum and everything it encompasses, at a methodological level, as well as at a mentality level.

Chapter One

The Basics – Recap of the Main Concepts

As mentioned in the introduction, the book at hand is meant to be a more in-depth approach to Agile project management, and, more precisely, and more in-depth approach to Scrum as a management method.

However, before we jump into the advanced notions and techniques needed to upgrade your Scrum project management game, we first need to go back to basics and do a little recap of everything you have learned until now (and everything that needs to be refreshed).

Therefore, this chapter has been dedicated to doing exclusively that: reiterating some of the basic concepts you may be familiar with, so that we can plunge into the deeper techniques of Scrum and Agile Project Management.

How Project Management Is Categorized

As I was saying before, project management can be done in a thousand different ways and given the wide range of approaches and the hundreds of combinations you can make between them, *thousands* is not even an exaggeration.

Understanding the underlying characteristics of project management and the points that bring together most of the approaches is really important in understanding how Scrum works. More than that, it is quite important for those moments when you might find yourself in the situation to bring two or even more project management methodologies together.

To understand how project management schools of thought can be so essentially different, you should understand that there is no "right" or "wrong" approach. Some may work in some situations, while others might work in other situations, industries, and types of teams. And that is perfectly normal.

You simply cannot say about a project management methodology that it is the "best" or the "worst" in any way; they are different in nature, and they can work in different contexts to a higher or lesser extent. Even if you are the proponent of a given project management method, keeping your eyes and your mind open to other types of project management will keep you on your toes, capable of implementing the necessary adjustments to your chosen methodology when this is needed.

So, for the purpose of helping you understand the wider realm of project management theory, here are some of the most popular methodologies out there:

1. Agile. This is one of the most commonly used project management methods today particularly in software development industries and generally technical environments.

   Agile works where the project has to be iterative and incremental (or at least up to some extent). It is a project management method that relies on collaborative effort and self-reliance/ organization more than anything else.

   If you had to put Agile on the opposite spectrum of another project management method, that would be Waterfall. As you will see later on in this book, Waterfall can have major pitfalls which Agile comes to offer a solution to.

   As you will also see in the next section of this book, Agile is mostly connected to the twelve points of its manifesto: a series of rules that function both as organizational elements and background philosophy for this particular methodology.

2. Scrum. This is the main topic of the book at hand. Scrum is a project management method derived from the original Agile which brings improvement to it by enhancing its main philosophy with concepts like the Daily Scrum, for example.

    Same as any other Agile project management method, Scrum only works in teams that can be self-reliant and disciplined. Without these two qualities of a team as a group, Scrum might not be the best solution.

    Furthermore, Scrum is more suitable in cases when there is a significant degree of uncertainty and things can easily slip out hand. Because it works in incremental steps, Scrum will make it easier to fix issues and add new items to the backlog.

3. Waterfall. Of all the project management methods out there, Waterfall is the most common and is frequently the most unrealistic one as well. In its very simple form, Waterfall does not take into account a series of variables that might affect the good course of the project.

    On the other hand, however, Waterfall is simple to understand, making it a gateway methodology for many junior project managers and helping them understand the very basics of project management.

    Waterfall is, to the date, one of the most popularly used project management methods in the world, even in some of the larger corporations. For environments like that, it only makes sense to manage everything at the highest level and not split a requirement into multiple tasks, from a Scrum project manager point of view.

    However, even Waterfall and Scrum can be reconciled and brought together as a symbiotic system that will help you better manage the deliverables of a project.

4. Six Sigma. This is one of the most highly regarded project management methods out there. Widespread across various

industries but predominantly used in the automotive one, Six Sigma is complex, intricate, and simple at the same time.

As a general rule of thumb, Six Sigma is usually seen as a problem solving methodology, rather than a project management methodology per se. However, due to its nature and the structured way in which it approaches matters, Six Sigma tends to be popular across corporations in particular precisely because it shows a clear inclination towards documentation and procedural implementation.

5. Kanban. Although we will not discuss Kanban extensively throughout this book, it is still important that you are aware of it and its basic principles.

Same as Six Sigma, Kanban is a Lean project management methodology and also the same as Six Sigma, it is one of the officially accepted approaches that come under the "methodology" category as well. This status is somewhat debated in the other examples given here however, for the purpose of this book's explanation, we will refer to Scrum as a methodology. The reason I have chosen to do this is because it does provide a system of practices and techniques that can be applied in project management.

Going back to Kanban, it can be said that it is extremely similar to Scrum. Same as Scrum, Kanban is suitable for smaller teams who need to be agile and easily adaptable, which is also why it makes all the sense in the world that these methods are used in software project management.

The main difference between Kanban and Scrum is, aside from the terminology used within the two systems, the fact that Kanban is even more relaxed than Scrum. While both of these project management methodologies rely on the existence of a backlog, Scrum also adds specificities about the time frame in which a project or a chunk of a project should be finished in.

6. Lean. This project management approach is frequently used in manufacture, where quality becomes more than an issue related to satisfying the client and more of an issue that has the potential to endanger lives.

   The reason Lean project management fits into this industry so well is because it focuses a lot on removing waste and delivering a perfect product in the end. The five core principles of Lean project management are value (providing value to the customer), the Value Stream (how value is created at the different levels of the project), Flow (the cadence and the rhythm of a project's work), Pull (reducing the waste), and Perfection (delivering a fully functional product at the end of the project).

   Six Sigma is frequently connected to the world of Lean project management as a sub-branch of it. However, their approaches are slightly different and it is worth studying both of them should you decide to settle on any.

Over the course of this book, we will discuss how the first four of these project management methods are connected through the lens of Scrum, how they can be reconciled when different teams, on different project management methodologies work, and how Scrum can offer value to most of them when implemented as a secondary line of thought.

What Is Agile Project Management?

Put in very simple terms, agile project management is a project management approach (or, to be more term-specific, it is the project management *framework*) that relies on splitting a larger project into smaller bits (called iterations) and working them out one step at a time. In general, Agile project management is most used in the software development and IT industries, but the same basic concepts can be applied in any other industry.

Agile project management is all about 12 principles, as follows:

1. The product/ software/ service you are planning should be delivered early to the customer. If that cannot be done, it is preferable that smaller sections of the product are delivered to the customer on a rolling basis.

2. Asking for feedback from the customer is extremely important, even if a product is in its final development stage. The benefit of an Agile project management approach is that it will allow you to make changes to the product so that the customer satisfaction is improved (in the end at least).

3. If the product is delivered in batches, it is important that these batches are delivered at regular intervals.

4. Both business-minded members of the team and development-minded members of the team must work together throughout the project, to ensure a quality final product that will be delivered to the customer.

5. The development team must receive all the support it needs to make sure the job is done - and done well.

6. Meetings are important for the success of the end product. They shouldn't necessarily be long, but they should convey, in a nutshell, all the information the team needs to work effectively and efficiently.

7. The progress of your product development can be measured if you prepare working prototypes of the software in advance.

8. The pace of the project must be maintained in a steady state by all the parts involved in the development of the project: developers, users, sponsors, etc.

9. Attention to technical detail and excellent design will help you make your product better with every iteration.

10. The entire process must be as simple as possible. The time needed to comprehend and complete a task should be as

minimal as possible; so, in other words, your team should focus on simple tasks that can be done on a "one step at a time" basis.

11. The best teams are the ones that can organize themselves internally, without a project manager to constantly tell them what to do. In an ideal situation, the project manager should only intervene when the situation triggers a red flag of any kind.
12. Team members should be encouraged to reflect on what goes well and what doesn't, and they should try to find solutions to be more efficient in their work.

Of course, this only puts Agile project management in very small bites, but I believe it serves the purpose here, as this is only meant to be a refresher for those of you who are already familiar with both Agile project management in general and Scrum in particular.

What Is Scrum?

If Agile project management is a framework (and thus, more of a *theory* than a set of rules to apply in practice), Scrum is one of the methods used in Agile project management. Albeit not the only one (Kanban and Extreme Programming are two of the other popular Agile project management methods), Scrum tends to be easier to digest - both on the end of the development team and on the end of the project managers. Furthermore, Scrum is easier to adapt to other industries, outside of software development. As you will see in later chapters, Scrum can be adapted to other areas of activity as well.

One way to spot Scrum-managed teams is the lack of a team leader inside them. Because Agile project management is all about self-organization, Scrum, as a method intrinsic to Agile, will not rely on a hierarchical team leader to assign tasks to each of the team members. Instead, the team members will be self-reliant and they will spot and fix the issues together.

There are many advantages to using Scrum in your project management approach. One of them is connected to the fact that it is *humane* in many ways. For instance, when you have to deal with a very large project ahead of you, jumping right into it might feel like a lot to take on. Scrum, on the other hand, takes away the anxiety of looking at a large project and splits its main chapters into chunks that are easier to digest.

Furthermore, Scrum is also advantageous from a business standpoint. Whereas in more traditional project management frameworks and methodologies, you are mostly relying on speculations and predictions, in Scrum, you are creating your next steps based on the work that has been completed already. This is extremely valuable especially in the case of projects that might be unpredictable, such as the development of a brand new software, for example.

In terms of where Agile and Scrum meet on theoretical grounds, the situation can be compared to that of a family. If Agile is a parent, then Scrum (along with Kanban, Extreme Programming and others), are the children. Agile parents will educate its children into their own ways, but, in the end, the children will become adults with their own viewpoints of the world and over how things should or shouldn't be done.

In Scrum project management, there are two main roles: the core one(s) and the auxiliary (external) one(s).

The core roles are played by the Product Owner, the Scrum Master, and the Development Team. Sometimes, these are also referred to as the "pig" roles.

The auxiliary roles are played by those who might not have a specific, formal role in the development of the product, and whose involvement is rather sporadic. Examples here include the accounting/ financial team, managers, stakeholders, and so on. Sometimes, these are also referred to as the "chicken" roles.

What Does a Scrum Roadmap Look Like?

Creating a Scrum roadmap is all about the speed of the process. In Scrum, you don't take a lot of time to plan ahead everything; instead, you break it all down in manageable chunks that can be delivered, feedbacked, and improved as you go.

There are two main elements to consider when creating the Scrum roadmap for your project: the nature of the project and the nature of the company culture. About the first, it can be said that Scrum Agile project management can be fit into nearly any kind of project, as long as it's large enough to be broken down into separate chunks of deliverables.

About the latter element, it can be said that not all company cultures would be a good fit for Scrum. In general, you need self-reliant teams that do not work based in predefined assigned tasks from their hierarchical managers; and this is why Scrum might not work when the company culture is a very corporate one, with very clear roles assigned to every person in the chain of command. Scrum can, however, be adapted to be suitable for a smaller team within a corporation. For example, if a corporation needs to develop a software product and hires an in-house team, that team can use Scrum project management to develop the software and it can consider the hierarchical superiors of that team to be the client in terms of where deliverables go and where feedback comes from).

When creating a Scrum roadmap, you need to take into consideration a few questions:

1. What are the priorities of each initiative (i.e. chunk of project)?
2. When will you work on each initiative?
3. Are there any specific deadlines you need to make sure you hit along the way?
4. Are there any kind of internal or external dependencies you need to consider?

5. Which teams work on which initiatives?
6. Do the teams have the availability and capacity to handle each initiative?
7. Is there something you can do to keep the current team(s) as stable as you can?
8. If you cannot maintain stability, how will you reorganize your team(s)?
9. If you have to reorganize teams or build a new one, will you take the ramp-up time into account when planning the project?

Taking the answers to these questions into consideration, you will then have to move through several Scrum roadmap building steps:

1. Identify all the product requirements of the product you want to deliver;
2. Write down each product requirement on a sticky note;
3. Place each sticky note in a different category, according to its theme;
4. Prioritize the sticky notes/ product requirements (e.g. place the high-priority ones on the left of the board and the low-priority ones on the right of the board);
5. Flag up any kind of business dependency by adding an annotation/ extra note to the product requirements (where necessary);
6. Together with the development team, flag up any technical dependency as well;
7. Together with the development team, identify feasible and timely delivery dates for each requirement;
8. Adjust the order of the tasks/ requirements based on the identified dependencies and time estimates.

Scrum projects also use a series of terms to define elements of the project management process. These terms are important because they will help you narrow down the entire process to the aforementioned chunks of deliverables. The most important ones include the following:

1. Theme. These are the groups features you will include in the product roadmap. For instance, if your client has ordered a software application that includes Social Media Management, the Customer Relationship Management and the Content Management System, each of these groups of features will be a "theme" in the Scrum project management paradigm.

2. Features. These are the actual capabilities of the project. For instance, taking the aforementioned example, features of the Social Media Management system will include the ability to post on Facebook, the ability to schedule posts on Facebook, the ability to edit posts on Facebook, the ability to post on Twitter, to schedule posts on Twitter, to edit posts on Twitter, and the ability to manage multiple end customer accounts on all these parallels.

3. Epics. These are series of actionable requirements that have to be tackled by the development team in order to develop a product feature.

4. User stories. This is the smallest kind of requirement, but, depending on its priority, it can be included in the product log. Every user story is consisted of an integration or an action that needs to be considered when developing the product.

5. Tasks. These are the small steps that have to be taken by the development team in order to develop the user story.

6. Sprint. This is a work cycle (usually taking two to four weeks), during which the team works on a deliverable.

Throughout the development of a Scrum project, you will also have to consider several types of meetings and overviews:

1. The Daily Standup/ Daily Scrum. This is a daily meeting where each team member gets up and speaks about the things accomplished the day before, the things they are aiming to accomplish on the current day, and the potential roadblocks they might meet along the way.

2. Backlog grooming/ Storyline. This is a type of meeting/ overview that will help you ensure the next few sprints are ready for planning.

3. Scrum of Scrums. When the product developed is very large, the Agile project manager will most likely split it in a few teams. The Scrum of Scrums brings all the Scrums up to date in a single meeting.

4. Sprint planning meeting. This recurrent meeting takes place before a new sprint and ensures all the members of the team are on track with their epics, user stories, and tasks.

5. Sprint retrospective. This recurrent meeting takes place after a sprint is done and it puts in retrospect everything that went right and everything that went wrong with the sprint that has been delivered.

Obviously, these are Scrum project management basics in a nutshell. The entire framework of Agile project management and the Scrum methodology in particular are, of course, much larger and more complex.

I will dedicate the following chapters to helping you understand where Scrum project management stands in relationship to some of the more popular "traditional" project management methodologies and frameworks, namely the classic, traditional project management, and the waterfall method.

After that, I will help you understand why Scrum goes beyond the borders of computer software and IT projects and is slowly redesigning the way people in multiple (somewhat unexpected) industries are handling project management.

Further on, we will dive into some of the most common Scrum problem solving techniques, as well as some soft skills and mindsets you need to acquire and establish in order for Scrum to provide you with maximum efficiency, regardless of what kind of project you may have to deliver.

Chapter Two

Putting Agile Scrum in Relation to Traditional Project Management

If you have worked with traditional project management (either as a project manager or as a team member), you have probably noticed that it can be frequently much too "stiff" for modern-day requirements, and even more so for industries where being flexible and easily adaptable is important.

At their very core, both agile project management and traditional project management aim for the same goals, and they rely on the same very basic fundamentals, such as the fact that the entire team should know about the scope of a project before it progresses. Of course, there are different methods on how this scope will be tackled and distributed across the team as tasks, but the very basics should be known by the members of the team regardless of the project management framework or exact methodology.

The first moment a conventionally managed project starts to differ from an agile one is the moment you start to plan it. In traditional project management, the project will be planned from the beginning to the day of the delivery, and most often, some sort of traditional project management tool will be involved as well.

The End of the Project

The way the project is handled throughout its duration and at its end is quite different in conventional project management vs. Scrum. The

White Book and the Agile Retrospective are the most concluding examples in this sense.

In conventional project management, the end of a project phase or the end of the entire project comes with a so-called "White Book". This is a recording of everything that went wrong and everything that was done right throughout the project, based on interviews the project manager had with team members (not necessarily all of them).

There are several flaws in this practice which Agile project management, and more specifically, Scrum project management, fixes.

For instance, during the White Book the fact that not all of the team members are involved in the final discussion might lead to a unilateral point of view, or at least a point of view that does not encompass the entirety of what happened throughout the project.

Even more, the White Book is frequently difficult to access for future projects and it is frequently useless even when created at the end of a project phase because the learnings drawn from it come too late to be implemented in the project approach.

With the Retrospective, these issues are fixed. Since all the team members are involved in it, the Scrum Master can get a very good idea of what happened and what learnings the team can draw from the experience.

Even more, the Retrospective takes place at the end of each sprint (which means that it happens once in a two-to-four weeks' time). This also means that whatever learnings have been drawn from it can be applied for the duration of the project onwards.

Incomplete Tasks

Issues arise when comparing incomplete tasks in conventional project management and Scum as well. In the case of the first approach, a task (or any kind of activity) that is not complete becomes part of the backlog and affects the overall completion timeline percentages on the charts. In the case of Scrum, however, incomplete tasks are moved to the next sprint backlog. Although dependency information might not be fully available when this happens, the information can still be included in a spreadsheet or database.

Schedule, Budget, Quality

The project burndown chart is used in project management to plan the schedule of the tasks and deliverables, as well as the budget of the entire project. Even without the burndown chart, the project manager will still have to handle all these elements; the chart just makes the status of the entire project more visual, which can be useful both for the members of the team and for the upper management as well.

Both in the case of traditional project management and Scrum, the project manager will always have to consider the three main variances that can appear in a project: the time variance, the budget variance, and the quality variance.

There are, of course, multiple elements that affect these three elements: from the way the human resources are managed, the way the logistics are managed, and to the more technical aspects.

In this respect, Scrum project management does not alter the basic "triad" of conventional project management, but adds up to it by increasing the tempo both in the case of reporting and in the case of accomplishment. Consequently, this will increase the pace of the project and reduce the risk that the budget and schedule plans are overrun.

This high-paced environment helps the team achieve a sort of momentum that puts them on track to every sprint and ever deliverable, without the need of micro management or heavy handed management of any kind.

Time Management

Another major difference occurs when comparing time management in conventional project management and Scrum. In the case of the more conventional approaches, the time management usually relies (quite heavily) on the comparison between the schedule and the actual performance. Frequently, hour billing systems are used in this respect, to accurately capture the specific work breakdown structure of the entire team.

These systems are not perfect, though. Sometimes, they can incur latency in the way the time reporting and the actual schedule are brought together. Moreover, there is always the risk of including time that was charged by mistake in the schedule planning as well.

Because Scrum breaks down the specific tasks of a project in very small chunks, they are much easier to manage and control. The daily meetings help reduce latency issues and achieve a better view of what is attainable and what is not in a given amount of time. If issues arise, the response time is much shorter, precisely because the entire project is split into sprints and monitored on a daily basis.

To some who might not be used to Scrum, the frequency of the meetings might feel like the kind of issue that lowers the efficiency of the entire team. However, allotting very specific times for these meetings is essential to ensure the team can get back to work as soon as possible. For instance, the daily standup should not last for more than three minutes per person, and each of the team members should only ask three simple questions, as straightforwardly as they can possibly do it.

To draw a parallel, in conventional project management, the recurrent team meetings can be much more inefficient in terms of time. Late arrivals, the jokes, and the irrelevant talks can prolong the meeting and make both the project manager and the team members lose grip of what is essential for a healthy advancement of the project onwards.

Time boxing is a Scrum concept that can be incredibly valuable for the timely completion of every task. Basically, this practice means that every team member will have to use a countdown timer for the tasks they are working on. The use of these timers will eventually improve the cadence of the entire activity and will eventually lead to the completion of the tasks sooner (sometimes, even sooner than planned, precisely because the rhythm at which they are completed is well-monitored and follows a very specific timing). From routine tasks to complex tasks, every activity can be time boxed in Scrum.

Communication

The way communication is done in conventional project management is different from Scrum as well. With conventional project management, there might be a very detailed plan on how communication should be done. From defining the stakeholders to the way the information should be disseminated and how the project status should be presented, everything usually goes into strict documentation. However, most of the time, these rules are not necessarily followed, or at least not to the letter, making their entire development process feel like a waste of time for those in charge.

Furthermore, meetings are very strictly scheduled on a recurrent basis, and they are complemented by impromptu meetings between some members of the team, when last minute issues arise. While the recurrent meetings have their purpose, they are frequently very time consuming and even their preparation might be difficult, especially when different teams and members of the team are located elsewhere.

In the Scrum approach, however, meetings happen more frequently and thus, all the stakeholders enter a certain rhythm with regard to reporting and meetings. Furthermore, the daily meetings help all team members stay on track with everything; so when the larger meetings take place, they don't have to be as long (fewer explanations are required, and thus, less time is needed).

Breaking Down the Tasks

In traditional project management, the term "work breakdown structure" is used. In Scrum, the same concept is used, but with a twist. The main difference occurs in the way the different tasks are ordered based on their hierarchy.

In conventional project management, advanced software might be used for this. In Scrum, a simple spreadsheet can be used, with the tasks ordered in columns that go from left to right, with the items on the right to be handled during the current sprint. Scrum allows the team to break down the tasks to a more molecular level than traditional project management which helps, as mentioned above, with the tracking of the project and the control the Scrum Master has over the different elements.

When creating a hierarchy for the tasks in the backlog, it is important to consider four main factors: integration, assembly, test, and checkout. These factors will give a good idea on which tasks should come first in the sprint and which should be added to the following sprint as well.

Handling Requirements

In both traditional project management and Scrum, what matters most is the voice of the customer. From this, all the requirements will ensue and once the requirements are clear, the project manager (or Scrum Master) can break them down into various tasks for the different members of the team.

The main difference in handling requirements, aside from the actual way they are broken down, comes when the requirements change (which is a pretty big possibility, regardless of the nature of the project). Any alteration in requirements will alter the work breakdown structure but in the case of Scrum, this can be easier to implement, precisely because the project is split in smaller chunks (which, in turn, means that only a few weeks' worth of work will be altered).

On the other hand, in the case of conventional project management, it is more difficult to implement changes in requirements. The main reason this happens is because the planning is done for very large chunks of the project, and any small change will affect the entire course of the project. With Scrum, however, the different stages of a project are very small and they are not as interdependent, allowing changes to be easily slipped in without affecting future sprints to a degree that it might affect the budget, schedule, or quality of the final deliverable.

The Depth of the Work Breakdown Structure

As it has been reiterated until now in this book, one of the main advantages of using Scrum project management is the fact that it is more flexible, allowing both the project manager and the team to better adjust along the way and ensure a final product that is as true as possible to the initial planning.

Compare this to being an Apple aficionado or a PC aficionado, if you may. Apple's main strategy is that of providing end-to-end products (meaning that everything is either manufactured in house or by very strict standards enforced by Apple). This allows them to sell products that are fully ready to use, but frequently lack the modularity of a computer PC. With an Apple desktop, even if you do have the knowledge to spot a faulty element and replace it, you can't fully do it. With a desktop PC, however, you can spot the component that's not functioning properly and replace it with any other component on the market, as you please (as long as it fits the main structure and specifications of the other components in the computer, of course).

The same basic concept can be applied when comparing Scrum project management and traditional project management as well. With a more conventional approach, the entire project is planned end-to-end and thus, replacing any "faulty element" will affect the entire structure of the plan.

With Scrum, however, the project is split in different "modules" (called "sprints", as it was mentioned before). Indeed, the project is more granularly sliced, but this allows the project manager and the team to replace any kind of "faulty element" far more easily (or simply to replace an element that doesn't fit into the overall structure anymore due to a change in client requirements).

In Scrum, the project breakdown structure should naturally go deeper than in the case of conventional project management; you need to go as far as you need to be able to split all the tasks in appropriately planned sprints. Bear in mind, these sprints should only include the tasks that are *feasible* during that given time slot. So, if you have a two-week sprint, you should not try to cram more items into it. For that sprint, plan only the items and tasks that are *doable* in the given amount of time.

The molecules of a sprint can be as large or as small as you want them to be. Some tasks can be fixed in a matter of minutes, while others might take days to figure out. What is important, however, is that you split the larger tasks in chunks that are small enough to be scheduled in one sprint. So, for example, if your sprint will be two weeks and you have 10 tasks that will take one hour each and another task that will take 13 days, and the hierarchy of the tasks says that the smaller tasks must be done first, you will most likely have to split the larger task into smaller ones - enough to fit them into the 14-day sprint and only have micro-tasks going into the next sprint.

It is very important to keep in mind that sometimes, backlogs might be congested. This usually happens when teams (or even specific members of a team) take on more than they can chew by overestimating their ability to complete certain tasks. There are many reasons they may do this; sometimes, it's a plain and simple mistake, but other times, it's a deliberate choice based on the fact that they are trying to impress someone (usually, someone in the management).

When congested backlogs are spotted, it is extremely important to move the tasks or activities to the next sprint, so that the current sprint is fully completed by the time the next one begins.

Control and Command Over the Project

As it was also mentioned before, Scrum project management allows for better control of the deliverables, from all points of view: time, money, and quality alike.

It is essential that both the Scrum Master and the team members understand that "controlling" a project is not the same as making single-handed decisions that affect the energies within a team (most frequently, in a negative way).

The risk that control and command of a project affect the energy of the team is much higher in traditional project management. The most common reason this happens is because traditional project management leans more on line management than other types of project management. This means that all decisions have to be taken by a hierarchical superior. Consequently, things might happen a lot slower, precisely because there is quite a lot of wait time between the moment a question/ inquiry is submitted until it reaches the appropriate line manager. Furthermore, information might get lost in this process, leading to decisions that will eventually frustrate the team members.

In Scrum, most of the decisions are taken internally, within the teams, with no necessary approvals from the hierarchical superiors. Both the feedback and the actual distribution of the tasks and activities is done based on daily standups and on a clear understanding of where each team member is and where they need to go. Moreover, because the decision makers are also the first-hand "operators" of a task or activity, they are more inclined to take a decision based on all the information available.

The daily standups help not only with the minute organization of the project, but also help something that is frequently more important: the team's honesty and sincerity in what they do. These daily meetings make them more accountable both in the eyes of their peers and in their own eyes, and once they get used to this type of management, they are more inclined to be honest about what they can and cannot do.

Quality Issues

What happens quite frequently in traditional project management is that issues that might arise within the development phase of a project push the deadline of each task further, leaving far too little time for actual quality assurance actions, verification, and validation.

You will see this happening everywhere, with both clients and project managers setting the deadline above and beyond any other parameter of success, and releasing products that are faulty just because they want this to happen by a certain date.

This kind of problem is far less frequent when Scrum project management is used, precisely because the delivery is made in smaller chunks and the entire project is split in smaller iterations, so that everything can be managed more accurately. Because Scrum is more flexible, a Scrum Master will not be tempted to reduce the time allotted for the QA phase, leading to a better product from the point of view of the quality.

Risk Management

In an ideal world, everyone would do everything textbook style: from A to Z, following each step and each bullet point of a procedure to the heart.

In the real world, however, that happens far too rarely.

Conventional project management does not officially acknowledge this, and thus, does not adjust to the realities of running and delivering a project as it *happens*, not as it is *supposed to* happen.

Scrum management does that and adjusts to the reality. It does this on all parallels involved in both development and delivery.

Risk management makes no exception from this general rule. Ideally, the risk management phase of a project would be done at its inception, and the project manager would have to assess the things that could go wrong. In reality, however, assessing all the issues that might come along is rarely possible; even more so in larger software development projects, where bugs and technical issues could arise where nobody could predict it.

Conventional project management is not entirely wrong in this. There are, indeed, issues that cannot be predicted, especially when projects are complex and/or lengthy by nature. What conventional project management does wrong, however, is the way it manages the entire structure of the project. In the traditional project management paradigm, when an unexpected issue comes along, it unsettles the entire process onwards, leaving no room for flexibility and adaptability. This usually happens precisely because the project is managed in large chunks, rather than smaller ones, like in the case of Scrum.

That is precisely the improvement Scrum brings along. The daily meetings, combined with the sprint ones and with the entire structure of the project allow the team members and the project manager to adapt easily to new requirements and situations, while still adhering to sprint deadlines and overall deliverable deadlines.

Furthermore, in the case of traditional project management, the risks that pop along the way can have ramifications that will affect the deliverables for weeks and even months, depending on how large/small the project is. In the case of Scrum, however, these risks are have a much smaller impact; usually, they impact the next sprint and then the work can fall back into place on the pre-established cadence.

To compare this to day-to-day activities, think of the old Roman adage, *carpe diem* meaning, in translation, *seize the moment*. This is frequently misunderstood, in the sense that a lot of people apply it in the wrong contexts like a night out with their friends, for example. The Romans, however, applied it in everything, both the pleasant events of their lives and the less pleasant ones (i.e. their duties and responsibilities).

Scrum takes this saying and applies it in project management in a way that is true to the Roman culture: seizing the moment is, for Scrum Masters, all about working on what is happening *right now*, rather than looking too far into the future and planning it in an idealistic way.

There are two major elements that help Scrum Masters stay on track with everything:

1. The small deliverables and the granular split of the entire project;
2. The constant meetings.

We have already explained why the molecular planning of a project is better for the overall quality of the project, as well as how it can help a project manager (Scrum Master, in this case) adhere to both budgetary and time-related constraints.

The meetings, on the other hand, help reduce risk. Compare this to a common cold, if you may. If you start sneezing and you start treating your cold as soon as possible, it will not grow into something more serious, which would eventually have to be treated with stronger medicine over the course of a longer period of time.

Scrum project management helps you spot the signs and symptoms of a mistake and eradicate them while they are still small and easy to repair; that is precisely why risks are much smaller in Scrum. Going back to the common cold comparison, sneezing a few times will be annoying, but it will not render you useless. Not handling these symptoms early on, however, can lead to infections, fever, and health issues that will put you to bed and prevent you from moving on.

Daily meetings (or daily standups, if you prefer that term) are, in many ways, like a daily checkup of all the symptoms that might deter you from your path and focus. Knowing where you were yesterday and what you have to accomplish today, as well as the potential setbacks that might occur today will help you manage everything better, stay more focused, and apply the right "medicine" where needed.

Feedback Loops

It would be rather redundant to say that feedback is important. Regardless of what type of project you may be managing or working on, knowing your client's feedback is precisely what helps you ensure the final product will be up to their expectations.

In conventional project management, this can be an issue, because feedback loops happen far away from each other - so when a feedback round comes in from the client, you might find yourself in a situation where you have to delay the development of the next stages in the project just to implement the actions and changes pointed out by the client.

In Scrum project management, this issue is almost removed from your way. Scrum is all about splitting large projects in small parts, same as you would portion size a large cake into single serving slices to serve your guests with. Not only does this help with the internal management of a project, but it also helps with the deliverables.

Scrum allows you to deliver parts of the project to the client and get feedback right away. Since these elements are small, the implementation of the feedback will be smaller both in terms of time and human resources. So, even if a sprint deliverable is not that great, making the necessary changes to make it satisfactory to the client will take a shorter amount of time and it will not necessarily delay future sprints.

Dependencies

Understanding your project dependencies is crucial in planning it well (and being able to adhere to your plan).

Even when you are just a freelancer, knowing that you depend on certain elements (even if it's just your internet connection or your ability to pay the electricity bills) is extremely important in adhering to your deadlines and delivering the quality the client was promised.

Identifying dependencies in conventional project management is quite important, of course. However, they grow in importance when Scrum project management techniques are used, precisely because in this case, the tasks have to come in a logical sequence and they are interdependent (at least up to a point).

Some tasks might not be connected to any others that have to be tackled during the development of a product. In Scrum, these are called "hangers", and it is crucial for the Scrum Master to handle these well, especially in terms of priority. Since these tasks are not necessarily connected to any of the other tasks, they have to be treated as separate entities and only "pasted" back into the main project when done, without altering the work that has already been done on the product thus far. This is possible only when these hangers have no schedule or budget dependencies of any kind, otherwise, they have to be treated the same as a normal sprint or series of tasks would be treated.

Chapter Three

Scrum and the Waterfall Method

The Waterfall project management method is, by far and large, one of the single most common methods of project management used by managers in a wide range of industries and situations.

It is also one of the most simplistic ones, but not necessarily in the sense that it can be done at the snapping of a finger. The Waterfall method has its intricacies, same as every other project management method but the simplicity of its very basics make it the first choice, especially in companies and fields that have either been used to it already, or simply find themselves in the situation to adopt a clear and straightforward project management approach.

In the Waterfall method, the tasks appear in the pipeline in a linear way, and they are completed linearly as well.

While extremely common, the Waterfall method poses tremendous risks and it is flawed in its very nature, precisely because it is based on an ideal landscape, where all the tasks that come in will never be changed and all the completed tasks are perfect.

In reality, if you have worked in any kind of environment, industry, and position, things never happen as "robotically" as the Waterfall method would imply.

One of the first and most common reactions generated by a product whose development has been managed using the Waterfall method is the simple: *why can't these people ever get it right the first time?*

The reason "they cannot get it right the first time" is because improper and idealistic project management has been applied in the development of the product. When you anticipate risks only at a very high level, when you expect everything to go smoothly, and when you don't take into account bumps in the road, your final product will be flawed on multiple levels.

The burdens a Waterfall project manager has to bear are quite significant:

1. He/she has to schedule timelines that extend to months and even years. This kind of approach only works when you have all the data and the science set in stone, which is entirely unrealistic, given the high duration of the timeline itself.

2. He/she has to be absolutely certain the quality of the project deliverable will be impeccable regardless of whatever unexpected situations may come along the way. This would require a fail-safe quality system set in place, a system that would never be wrong in spotting the bugs (which is, again, unrealistic). Even more, the project manager would have to know with absolute certainty that any bug that pops up will be fixed in a very strict amount of time accounted for from the very beginning of the planning phase.

3. He/she has to be absolutely certain all team members will fully understand their roles, their tasks, and that they will work at maximum efficiency throughout the entire duration of the development phase. Even more, the project manager will have to be absolutely certain that the team will stay the same throughout the development and quality checking phase, and given the high mobility of the workforce in the IT industry (and any other industry, really), this is entirely unrealistic as well.

In some cases, the Waterfall method might be used in a slightly more sophisticated version, where loop backs are planned for in the eventuality of a stage gate cannot be moved through. This is, of course, more realistic than the simple Waterfall approach, but it still poses significant issues, including:

1. The long term planning still lies at the very foundation of the entire project. As it was discussed in the previous chapter, this could bring along a series of problems including the inability to stick to a clear deadline, to deliver quality, or to adhere to a given budget.

2. The resources, be them human resources or other types of resources, have to be there for at least the duration of the project as it was initially scheduled, preferably for more time (in case drawbacks move the deadline further on). As mentioned above, this can be an issue particularly in those industries where work stability is a huge issue that sets back entire companies.

Are There Benefits to Using the Waterfall Method?

Well, yes.

If you read any of the paragraphs in this chapter so far, you might be tempted to believe that the Waterfall method is flawed "to the bone". However, if it were so problematic, people would not continue to use it, which they do, including in some software development companies, for example.

The single most beneficial aspect of the Waterfall method is the fact that it is easy to understand. So, in theory, it might work OK for smaller projects or project managers who are just starting out in their line of activity.

It is important to comprehend the fact that just because the Waterfall method is easy to understand in theory, it doesn't mean that its application is equally easy. It goes the other way around, actually. As a theoretical method, the Waterfall approach will make it extremely easy for you to understand the basic concepts behind project management and what it involves. In practice, however, the Waterfall method can lead to major issues along which will make the entire management process of a project feel a lot slower, more twisted, and generally speaking, more difficult.

I will draw a parallel with a literary work that has been long known to be associated with pure optimism: *Candide*, by Voltaire. In this book, the main (eponymous) character has to face a series of struggles, but his motto is "We live in the best of the possible worlds". [1]

If you know Voltaire, you know this entire story is written ironically. If you are not familiar with his work, you might take this as an inspirational book and place it at the center of everything you do, including project management.

The major flaw of the Waterfall method is precisely this: living in the best of the worlds. In other words, overly-optimistic expectations on all the elements of a project's development lie at the very basis of the Waterfall method.

Scrum and Waterfall?

Scrum project management might seem irreparably far from the Waterfall method, but they can actually be reconciled, with Scrum being precisely what the Waterfall method is missing: realism.

The major pitfall of the Waterfall method is the fact that it "judges" everything from the prism of the larger picture. Don't get me wrong here: having the larger picture in mind is essential when you manage a project of any nature, any duration, and using any project management framework or methodology on the planet. However, solely seeing the larger picture doesn't make you a project manager: it makes you, maybe, a great strategist in an ideal world, but it does not help you ensure the quality, timeliness, and budget-friendliness of the final deliverable.

Given the idealistic expectations of the Waterfall method, it might thus be surprising to some if I tell you that the Scrum methodology is

---

[1] ALMA CLASSICS.(2018). *CANDIDE*.[S.l.].

nothing but a variation on Waterfall, one that eliminates the quintessential flaw in the entire approach, though.

Scrum takes the Waterfall method and applies it to smaller elements of the project. As we have mentioned before, these smaller elements account for different features of a product and they are developed during short-term project sprints that take up to two weeks.

By eliminating the long-term project management paradigm from the Waterfall method and replacing it with a granular approach, the major issues of this methodology are eliminated as well, and the risks that come with it too.

How are the Waterfall and the Scrum methods so similar?

At their very core, they are both based on linearity and the congruence of the tasks within a project. However, planning the long run based on this philosophy will eventually lead to (maybe irreparable) damage to the budget, timeliness, and quality control of the final product. Planning the short sprints, however, puts everything in an entirely new perspective, allowing you to micro-manage problems when they appear, for the sake of the final deliverable.

Is Scrum always a good idea?

Yes, and no. Most of the theoreticians in this field will agree that Scrum is a realistic approach that makes sense for most industries and types of products and projects.

Issues may arise when a team that uses the Scrum method tries to work with a different team, that uses the Waterfall method. In this situation, the latter group may not fully understand the granularity of what the first group is trying to do and thus, they might not understand how everything will come together.

The main way to fix this issue is to ensure that every sprint will lead to a usable product/ feature. This way, the team using the Waterfall method will fully understand the way the final product is being built and they will be able to interact with each sprint deliverable on their own terms, using their own project management method.

Are there any situations when Scrum is definitely not OK to use?

Most definitely yes. It is far from the purpose of this book to glorify Scrum as the one and only project management methodology, and I do not intend to do that. There are, of course, situations when other project management approaches are far better than Scrum.

For example, Scrum may not be a very good option where self-discipline is an issue. People might find it difficult to admit this to themselves, both regarding their own actions and regarding those of their team members. However, using a Scrum methodology with an undisciplined team can only lead to major problems, which may or may not culminate with the failure of an entire project deliverable.

Furthermore, in large corporations where procedures are very often followed down to the small print, Scrum may not be a very good approach. It can work for smaller teams within a corporation as long as Scrum is implemented as an "underground" methodology, but it might not be a good fit for the way corporations function. The micro-management of Scrum could turn into a big disadvantage in these types of companies precisely because they have to handle hundreds, if not thousands of tasks on a daily basis. So narrowing and splitting them down to even more tasks might make management extremely difficult at all levels, from the upper management to the project manager of the smallest team in the company.

Scrum tends to work best in smaller companies and startups that are still shaping the way they work and are open to new approaches. Although, of course, very similar in nature to every other project management methodology out there, Scrum can be a little "too new" for companies where teams and project managers are already very used to working on traditional methods or even the simplistic Waterfall method itself.

How to Implement Scrum in Skeptical Teams

When team members have been used to a specific methodology (but it is not entirely ingrained in the way they think and perceive work), it is easy to understand why they might be skeptical to embrace a completely new approach: one that requires them to give daily updates and stay true to their capacities in every way there is, for that matter.

In these situations, skepticism may be a problematic issue because, in the end, Scrum is about getting everyone on board with an entire mindset, rather than just a methodology on how to approach tasks, projects, and deliverables.

When doubt clouds the mindset of even just a couple of team members, it can extend like a plague and it can make everyone else question the achievements of Scrum project management. Moreover, it can lead to actual resistance and even sabotage from the team members.

If you see this type of behavior in your team members, it is extremely important to get the upper management on board with your way of seeing things. This way, team members will eventually give their vote of confidence for the new approach you are bringing forward.

Bringing Together the Waterfall Method and the Scrum Method

If you have decided to implement Scrum as a complement to your already implemented Waterfall method, you will have to take several reconciliation points into consideration. These points may or may not pose a challenge, but even if they do, they consist of matters that must be tackled as soon as possible, so that you lay a smooth ground to build your Scrum on.

Here are some of these reconciliation points:

Prepping the Basis

From the outside, Scrum may seem a very loose way to deal with serious projects but, as you will see later on, this project management method is anything but that; in fact, it is so solidly grounded in discipline that it can even be applied to the military industry (or at least branches of it, where planning and project management are necessary - such as the building of various defense mechanisms, for example).

So, it is completely understandable if team members are highly skeptical about the promises of Scrum and whether or not it works. Some may see it as too relaxed, others might be downright irritated by the constant reporting they have to do, but in the end, most of the teams standing on either of these fences admit that Scrum is everything they didn't think it would be and that it helped them grow professionally.

Going back to the reconciliation points I was mentioning above, before you dive into any kind of implementation of the Scrum approach, you should first make sure the grounds are ready. You wouldn't build a house on unprepped terrain, so why would you try to implement a new project management approach on muddy waters?

So, to make sure everyone is on the same page in terms of the Scrum basics, it is highly recommended that you train them and help them acquire the terminology and the practices of this project management method. To be more specific, you need to make sure the following training points are fully done before you deploy Scrum:

- What Scrum and Agile project management and development are
- What are complex adaptive systems (and how they fit into the landscape of your team's work)
- What are the main roles in a Scrum team (Scrum Master, Product Owner, Team Member, Stakeholder, Manager)
- The main types of meetings (Sprint Planning, Sprint Review, Sprint Retrospective and the Daily Scrum)
- The main types of documentations (Backlog and Burndown Chart)

- How a project plan looks (introducing the team to concepts like Project Schedule, Project Reviews, and Project Milestones)

Do not expect all of your team members to fully understand what Scrum is all about if they have not heard of it before or if they don't even have acquaintances who might work on this model. It would be unrealistic for you to expect your entire team to know what is expected of them after just a few sessions of training, with no actual practical experience in this new "game".

Furthermore, when deploying the Scrum methodology for the same time, it is of the utmost importance that you take it step-by-step. Basically, the first few sprints are all about understanding the way Scrum works and its basic concepts, more than anything else. For this reason, the first couple of sprints will most likely be consisted of planning activities.

Furthermore, once Scrum has been deployed, it is also important to make sure you analyze the post-deployment essentials in a meeting with all of your team members, as well as adjacent teams that might still work based on the Waterfall method.

Why invite those teams to the meeting as well?

Mostly because this meeting is meant to help you reconcile any kind of issues anyone, from your team or another team, has spotted along the way and to make the necessary amendments. Generally, this meeting is to take place about two months into the deployment of Scrum, so that people have enough time to see how it works and what could be improved. This way, both your team and the teams they are interacting with will be able to construct valuable, actionable feedback, rather than just toss a mere "I don't like it".

One of the most important points you should touch upon in this meeting include how the teams feel about the following:

- The schedule review
- The budget review

- The quality issues
- The milestones that were accomplished
- The metrics connected to value
- When the next meeting will take place
- (For the Scrum team) the Sprint Reviews, overall project metrics, verification, and validation.
- (For the Waterfall team) the in-process reviews, the overall project metrics, the verification, and the validation.

Furthermore, this meeting should help you determine how to bring together the Scrum team and the Waterfall team in a cohesive and realistic way. For this to happen, this meeting should answer the following goals:

- Coordinate the sprint team results with the overall plan
- Coordinate the waterfall team results with the overall plan
- Determine if there is a gap between the two teams
- Determine how to eliminate the gap and create documentation to attest to this

Risk Management

As it was touched upon in the previous chapter, risk management is easier when using Scrum, precisely because this methodology is based on a short framed horizon. Consequently, this minimizes the uprising of major issues that take a lot of time and resources to be handled and ensures the project deliverables will fit within the time, budget, and quality frame of the client requirements.

In most cases, the risk management approach of Waterfall can be implemented quite easily into the Scrum methodology. Namely, whatever you were doing in Waterfall will be applied in Scrum as well, but to a shorter duration and a more realistic mindset.

Communication

One of the greatest advantages of the Scrum project management approach is the fact that communication happens on a very frequent basis (daily!).

In the case of a team that uses the Waterfall approach, however, communication may not be quite as frequent as it should be and thus, there might be a communication gap between Scrum teams and Waterfall teams that need to work together.

The so-called "Big Meeting" is a meeting that takes place halfway through the duration of a project (or more frequently if the project is meant to last for a very long period of time) and its main purpose is that of helping Scrum teams and Waterfall teams communicate with each other.

Implementing something as granular as the Daily Standup in a Waterfall team is not necessarily a good idea if they need to stay on the same method. Doing so would actually push them towards becoming a Scrum team; As mentioned before, this might not work in all situations, and even if the potentiality of Scrum functioning for them is really high, the deployment should be done gradually, not through the force implementation of a daily meeting.

Milestones, Gates, and Sprints

What is essentially called "Sprint" in Scrum project management is a milestone or a gate in other methodologies, including the Waterfall method. The main difference is, however, that Sprints are smaller milestones - baby steps, if you want to put it like that - while the Gates and Milestones accepted in the more traditional project management methodologies are much larger.

The reconciliation of these differences is mostly connected to terminology. A milestone can be split into several Sprints, for example. So when reporting is done, the Scrum team will report that a Milestone was achieved, rather than 10 smaller Sprints.

It is, however, important that both teams are at least familiar with the terminology of each of the project management methods used. This will help them better understand where everyone is standing and it will make communication easier within the teams and among them as well.

Verification and Validation

This might be one of the more difficult parts in reconciling a hybrid between Scrum and Waterfall teams, mostly because some timing discrepancies might arise between the two teams.

One of the best ways to deal with this is to use a TEMP (Test and Evaluation Master Plan) approach. TEMP is a term borrowed from homeland security terminology, but which can very much function in all sorts of industries as well.

Basically, what this implies is creating a procedure that can be applied to both types of teams seamlessly, eliminating risks on both sides as well. It is highly recommended that this procedure is constructed based on the criteria the product/ deliverable has to meet in order to be satisfactory; and for that to happen, the project manager has to be more than familiar with the dependencies of the project and what they actually implied.

Overall, Waterfall and Scrum can work together, both as a hybrid within the same team and as different teams that have to work for a common goal. It's not an easy reconciliation, despite the major similarities between the two approaches, but even so, it can be done.

It is of a massively crucial importance that you set the grounds correctly from the very beginning if you want to make sure the entire experience will not be a fiasco: one that will delay the deliverables and set your team as far from Scrum as possible, for that matter. With good planning and an open mind, the reconciliation is more than possible, but there is a certain amount of work that goes into this, so you absolutely need to take it into account as well.

Chapter Four

Implementing Scrum Management as a Line Manager

In the previous chapter of this book, I showed you how to reconcile two project management methods that might seem to stand at opposite sides of the spectrum, but which can be harmoniously brought together under certain circumstances.

I was also mentioning that implementing Scrum might not be the best idea in larger corporations, where the standards and procedures are very closely followed and where most of the managers (project managers and upper managers alike), as well as the employees are already accustomed to a given type of project management.

However, I was also saying that you can sometimes use Scrum project management in these organizations as long as you do it at a more local level, with teams that are smaller and perhaps more open to this kind of implementation.

This is where the current chapter will come in handy. If you are a line manager and would like to implement Scrum project management in your team, regardless of what the other teams in your company might be using in terms of methodology, this chapter is for you.

This type of Scrum deployment can prove to be actually useful and it can help the entire company stick to its given deadlines, even if not all the teams in a development project adopt Scrum as their main project management methodology.

In order for your attempt to function and coordinate well with the rest of the company, it is quite important that you take it gradually from the very beginning.

For instance, to begin with, once your team has been accustomed to the basic concepts and terminology behind Scrum, you could start by using it on projects that are near to completion for the first sprint. This will help you and your team determine how Scrum works and how to make it efficient for your particular dynamic.

In this given scenario, adopting Scrum will eventually help you move through tasks that have been lagging for some time and still make sure that the smaller tasks are accomplished as well. Therefore, the Scrum deployment will eventually help you move the entire project closer to completion.

Aside from the type of projects you should choose to implement Scrum with at the beginning, there are several other factors you should consider. Taking these factors into your plan will help you coordinate with the line management and prove that Scrum can be an efficient methodology for your team.

To be able to deploy Scrum correctly and see the results you are expecting, it is important to make a fair assessment of the performance, both at an individual level and at a team level.

To do this, you should:

1. Pinpoint the scope of the project or activity. In other words, determine the actual objectives of an activity. This should be done together with the team and it should help everyone understand what the main goal is. In Scrum, the scope of the project is relayed in the backlog.
2. Collect the evidence necessary to make an assessment. This step is all about assessing the progress of a project. In Scrum, this is done mostly through the Daily Standups, where each team member self-assesses their activity and the potential roadblocks.

3. Engage the assessed individual or team. Keeping the team members in the loop with the reviews helps them achieve better performance, precisely because they are aware of the elements that might be faulty in their activity. Daily meetings, as well as the Sprint reviews, plannings, and retrospectives all play an engagement role for the team, allowing them to stay in touch with everything that happens on a project.

4. Coach them and help them in the understanding of given KPIs (key performance indicators). If you are a line manager, it is quite likely that you will have to do some coaching with your team members as well. This is perfectly understandable and acceptable, given the nature of the situation. However, it is also quite important that you don't do these coachings during the Daily Meetings, or anytime public. It is better to schedule private sessions for this; it is more productive both for the coachee and for the entire team to do it this way.

5. Evaluate the results of their work. The evaluation should check the team results against what was initially planned. This can be done at an individual level (e.g. if a team member has managed to deliver all the Sprints correctly and in time), or it can be done at a team level (assessing if the entire team has reached the planned goals).

All of these concepts are at least vaguely familiar to anyone in any kind of environment, regardless of whether they have used Scrum before or not. Most companies evaluate their employees based on given KPIs and want to provide them with all the tools to succeed including coaching, engagement, and so on. Therefore, when you move to a Scrum approach, your team members will be somewhat familiar with the evaluation procedures; they will just have to adjust to these evaluations happening more often than what they are used to.

The main challenge of a line manager when implementing Scrum is making sure the team will eventually become self-directed - meaning that they will not take "orders" from you any longer. Instead, they will be self-sufficient and work based on their own targets, building discipline and stronger work ethics. This can be done only by changing the mindset of the entire team which, as you will see later on, is more about the soft skills of the Scrum Master/ project manager/ line manager and about the "extras" the company can provide, rather than being about any kind of procedure.

Furthermore, a thorough understanding of how the backlog works is quite important when moving from traditional line management to Scrum management as well. Your team should look at this backlog as a pool of small tasks that need to be directed into the correct sprint in order for them to make a difference for the final deliverable at the end of the project.

There are, of course, software applications and internet browser tools that help create a comprehensive backlog, but since you might not have the budget or the approvals to implement these already, a simple spreadsheet will make do. Keep in mind, though: spreadsheets can only work up to a point. Beyond that point, the large number of tasks in the spreadsheet might make it difficult to operate and downright chaotic for anyone looking at it, even for yourself, as the Scrum Master who has generated the spreadsheet and participated in any change occurring in it.

Once the backlog and the concept of a Sprint are fully understood by a team, they will slowly start to understand the importance of being self-reliant and honest (both with themselves and with the other team members). Therefore, deploying Scrum project management as a line manager will become far easier, and you will be able to submit reports to your own hierarchical superiors that show actual results and coordinate with the goals of the company as a whole.

Chapter Five

Scrum Problem Solving Techniques

Even if you don't decide to adopt Scrum entirely, there are still many ways it can be useful to you and your team. For instance, if you use a specific project management approach and stumble upon a complex issue that needs to be fixed as soon as possible, you can deploy Scrum as a project management methodology for that specific problem.

This can work in a variety of contexts and Scrum can be a problem solving technique in its own right precisely because it is a small task oriented project management method and it will allow you to make fast progress on the development of a solution for a problem.

To prove that Scrum can be integrated as a problem solving technique, we will move through its relationship to Six Sigma (one of the most common project management techniques out there), as well as how it relates to The 8 Disciplines (also known as the 8Ds) and the so-called Five Whys.

1. Scrum vs. Six Sigma: The Perfect Couple

If Waterfall is the most popular project management method due to its hassle-free perspective on what needs to be done (and how), Six Sigma is one of the most elevated and complex project management methods.

There are entire schools of thought, courses, lessons, and even ranks within the Six Sigma project managers, making this one of the most common approaches in companies that want to accurately and correctly manage their projects, but cannot rely on Scrum only.

Like Scrum, Six Sigma is frequently used in software development companies and the first can be a very good complement to the latter, precisely because they are quite similar in nature.

Since this book is not mainly focused on Six Sigma, I will only brush upon what it means and how it can be integrated with Scrum. I believe this will be of great help for those of you who are already working as Six Sigma project managers, but who are tempted by the advantageous proposals Scrum is making as well.

Since both Sigma and Scrum are quite similar at their very core, bringing the two together should be fairly effortless as long as you understand the correlation between them as methodologies, as well as the main differences that set them apart.

The Roles

Six Sigma roles are quite famous in the project management circles, mostly because there is a heavy association between them and the way martial arts are structured within a school of thought. This has, of course, quite a lot of ramifications in terms of the philosophy behind Six Sigma, but as mentioned before, since this is not a book dedicated to this specific project management approach, I will not go in depth on that specific branch of what Six Sigma is.

There are several roles that have to be defined when talking about Six Sigma. Usually, the Champion is the person (or group of persons) lying at the top of the hierarchy - the executives, if you want to speak in corporate terms.

Furthermore, the Champion guides the Black Belt and the Green Belt managers who are the representatives of the mid to upper management in the case of a corporation, depending on its specific structure and goals.

Most often, the Black Belt and the Green Belt managers will be the ones managing the projects, so it makes sense that either both or just one of them will be assigned with the Scrum Master role when Scrum is deployed within their team(s). Ideally, the Champion will also be the

Scrum Master but more often than not, the people managing a company (be it large or small) at executive level do not have the time for daily meetings and cannot commit to this fundamental concept in Scrum management.

How Six Sigma Works

When it comes to Six Sigma management, a lot of emphasis is put on training - all the roles at the top of the organization need to be fully trained in understanding the basic concepts behind their chosen project management method. Some of the most important concepts they need to understand include the following (not necessarily in the order they will be approached when applied on an actual project):

- Definition
- Recognition
- Analysis
- Measurement
- Improvement
- Standardization
- Control

These concepts are very important in Six Sigma because the entire project management methodology relies a lot on statistical data gathered throughout the duration of a project (or of a previous project), and which has to be categorized under the correct concept.

Each of these concepts stands for a crucial project management phase, making the understanding of the terminology even more important. The phases of a Six Sigma project are as follows:

Recognition

This is not a phase per se, but a moment of realization - the realization that a new project needs to be started. This moment might come when an order is placed by the customer, but it might as well come when a corporation notices that there is a pain point they can, and should, fix.

Definition

This phase will officially formalize the existence of a project and its main meta-data. This is the phase in which a team is brought together and it is also the phase usually correlated with the concept of "scope management" in traditional project management.

During the Definition phase, the Champion, the Black Belts, and the Green Belts define the goal of the project, the problem it needs to fix, and the direction in which the project should go.

Once the actual goal of a project has been defined, the managers need to define the project charter as well. In Scrum, this concept is somewhat similar to that of the product backlog, meaning that the entire project will be split in different elements which will be handled as more or less individual, but correlated entities.

Measurement

This is the phase that is usually connected to the KPI setting stage in a more traditional project management approach. Once the scope of the project has been defined, the Black Belt, the Green Belt, and perhaps even the Champion have to establish the metrics that have to be considered when applying to that scope.

Analysis

Once the main data of a project has been collected, the managers will have to analyze it. In Scrum management, this is the point where the team uses statistical tools like Pareto charts to spot the most important pieces of information and use them to find a solution to a given problem. Once the solution has been established, it will become part of the backlog as one item or as multiple items in one or more Sprints, depending on how large or small the given problem or requirement may be.

Improvement

Analysis will provide you with the theoretical solution - but it is during the Improvement phase that the team will work on implementing that situation. With Scrum, the implementation can be more seamless than with the more traditional project management approaches. The reason this happens is because Scrum will split the problem into smaller tasks - so if any kind of bumps in the road set back the entire project, you can easily smoothen out those bumps and move on with the implementation of your solution.

Control

Contrary to what it might sound like, the Six Sigma Control phase has nothing to do with micromanaging your team and exasperating them with following their every move. In fact, it has everything to do with making sure the improvements implemented in the previous stage are sustainable on the long term.

This is similar to spotting a spice or a herb you don't like in food. Once you have determined what it is, you will make sure you don't add it to your dishes from thereon. It is, of course, an ultra-simplistic comparison - but the main idea behind it can be very well applied to the Control phase in Six Sigma project management as well. More specifically, if you have spotted an issue and if you have delivered the solution for that issue, you will want to make sure the problem will not be repeated and that it will affect the project onwards. In other words, once this task is done, it should be done forever and you shouldn't have to implement the same solution all over again should a new similar task/ problem arise.

Standardization

One of the main reason Six Sigma project management works in larger companies, and even monster corporations, is because it actually formalizes all the procedures. So, once a problem has been fixed and once a pattern of avoiding it has been created, all you have to do is to standardize it; create a procedure of improvements that have to be done and actions that have to be taken in order for the problem to be avoided in the future.

Six Sigma and Scrum might seem severely different in nature, especially with the Six Sigma's inclination towards corporate culture and standardization, and with the frequent association between Scrum and startup businesses.

However, they are very easy to reconcile, easier than the Waterfall method and the Scrum method, actually. Once you move past the terminology and the philosophy surrounding Scrum and Six Sigma, you will discover that they are very close at core, and that you can coordinate the concepts of one to the concepts of another without issue. Even more, the mindset of a Six Sigma team is very similar to that of a Scrum team, allowing you to "marry" the two in a way that is actually harmonious.

Scrum and Six Sigma Integration

Both Six Sigma and Scrum pertain to apparently different worlds. The first one is a Lean project management framework, and the latter is an Agile project management framework.

Where the Six Sigma seems almost dogmatic in the steps it makes towards the completion of a project, Scrum feels like a joke to anyone who hasn't tried it. In the end, it is in Agile environments that the whole "play area in the work space" idea has occurred, so it makes all the sense in the world that the sometimes austere adopters of Six Sigma might feel skeptical when faced with the disarming openness of the Scrum methodology.

The two of them can come together, though. Even more importantly, they come together on a pretty frequent basis these days, and they complement each other down to the smallest bit.

To understand how the two of them come together, you must first understand that they do not lie on the opposite ends of the spectrum, as it may happen with conventional project management and Scrum, for example.

In fact, they are quite close, as they both focus on constant improvement. Six Sigma is a problem solving framework, more than anything else. It focuses on determining issues and on finding solutions for those issues that will be implemented both at that given moment, and in the future (for the prevention of the issue).

Scrum, however, is a philosophy of work.

Where Six Sigma fails to bring teams together in a cohesive way, Scrum manages to do that. Moreover, where Scrum fails to spot issues, find solutions, and avoid the repetition of a mistake, Six Sigma manages to bring in just the right amount of "corporate culture" and predisposition to strategy and procedure to ensure the correct fixing of that issue.

The main challenge and the main bridge you will have to build between Six Sigma and Scrum is that of the incremental approach. Six Sigma does not necessarily split the requirements of a project in such small bites as Scrum does. However, it can definitely incorporate that into its MO as well, without any kind of issue.

The major elements of Six Sigma (Recognition, Definition, and so on) can be coordinated into a Scrum backlog just as they would normally. Once implemented there, however, they will have to be sliced down to manageable chunks and assigned appropriately.

Scrum is a perfect Six Sigma overlay, the same way a leather jacket will always look good over a simple, austere white T-shirt. Basically, when bringing together these two approaches, you will be managing your projects using the Six Sigma structure, but you will apply the essential Scrum elements into the mix: the backlog, the iteration of small tasks, the Daily Scrum, and so on.

2. Scrum vs. The Eight Disciplines: The Close Siblings

The Eight Disciplines are a problem solving approach that can be applied to most project management methods, as the steps to solving the issue are easy to correlate with the stages of any project management style.

To put things in a bit of perspective and correlate it with what this book has taught you so far, The Eight Disciplines can be applied to the Waterfall method just as well as they can be applied to the Six Sigma method; both of them are more or less on different ends of the project management theory pole in the sense that one is very simplistic and the other one is rather intricate.

Scrum makes no exception from this rule. The Eight Disciplines and Scrum can come together to solve problems that need to be handled as speedily and as correctly as possible.

To understand why the two can go hand-in-hand so well, it is important to understand the disciplines themselves and how they tie into problem solving as a mindset.

Basically, The Eight Disciplines refer to eight stages of problem solving that should be applied, as follows:

1. Select your team to help you with the situation. It is important to make sure the team has the expertise to spot the problem, its source, and to find an adequate solution.

2. Define the problem according to The Five W's. This is not to be mistaken with the Five Whys, which is a slightly different approach to problem solving - one which we will get into a bit later on into the book (next sub-chapter). For now, we will resume to explaining that The Five Ws are *Who, What, Where, When,* and *Why*. They are frequently accompanied by *How Many* and *How* as well (which transforms the whole concept into "the 5W2H"). Asking these questions will help you define the main issue at hand, and it can also help you determine a solution later on.

3. Develop a plan to help you make sure the problem is contained - specifically, that the problem is kept away from the customer in every respect. The end client does not need to know about the problem, as long as you are actively working on solving it.

4. Spot and verify the root cause(s) of the problem. This is extremely important because it will help you avoid it in the future. Furthermore, determine potential escape points as well: the moments that changed the course of the project and allowed the problem to appear. Keep in mind that the identification of the problem root(s) and its escape points should not be a mere brainstorming; it should also include a thorough verification process that will allow you to know, 100%, why a problem occurred.

5. Spot corrections and verify them. These corrections should have a permanent nature, in the sense that they should be applied in a way that will prevent future similar issues to appear. The corrective actions for a problem or nonconformity should be verified by using quantitative research and confirming that the implementation of the solution will prevent future problems to stand in the way.

6. Implement the corrective actions. Once you have verified that a proposed corrective action is the right one, it is time to implement it. And once *that* is done as well, you should verify that the problem has been completely fixed as well.

7. Discuss preventive measures. This stage is very important because it will help your team prevent future problems of a similar nature. Wherever needed, adapt the management systems, practices, and procedures of the company to include these preventive measures.

8. Formally thank the team. This step might not be on your mind when you are in a rush to make sure you fix an issue, but it is extremely important for the course of your collaboration with

the team members, as it will acknowledge their collective effort and make them feel involved in the success of a team.

OK, so where does Scrum come into play in all this?

You can pretty much apply the Scrum methodology throughout the entire problem solving process and treat it as a separate, adjacent project that acts as a dependency for the main one. Obviously, the "Discipline" where Scrum will function the best is the implementation phase, especially when it's something that might be lengthier. Implementing Scrum here will help you make sure everyone is on track both with their main Sprints and with their problem fixing ones. Of course, you will also need to adjust future sprints to factor in the time needed to implement the problem solving solution.

When it comes to the other Disciplines in this problem solving approach, you may not fully rely on Scrum, as they are frequently related to discussions and brainstormings. However, you can implement Scrum in the verification process, and you can implement Daily Standups to see where the team members are in spotting the problem, the cause, and the solution.

You can look at The 8 D's and Scrum from the other point of view as well: that of a quality assurance team that is already managed by a Scrum Master. In this case, The 8 Disciplines become the integration, by helping the team members with their Daily Standups and with the final deliverable of a solution. Applying a problem solving methodology like this will help them stay disciplined and true to the nature of the tasks they have to accomplish on a daily basis, and it will give them a structure to help them stay on track with how the problem is solved, implemented, and then prevented in the future.

Overall, there is absolutely no reason why The Eight Disciplines and Scrum will not work together, regardless of which end of the spectrum you look from. The two approaches come from different realms of thought, but they can be reconciled with absolutely no issue in terms of mindset and procedure. The 8 D's will not affect the structure of the Scrum project in a negative way, and the Scrum methodology and mindset will fit perfectly into the 8 Discipline paradigm as well.

3. Scrum vs. The 5 Whys: The Friendly Neighbors

Same as The 8 D's, the 5 Whys are not a project management approach per se, but a problem solving approach that can be implemented in the grander scheme. Even more, as it was shown before, the 5 Whys can be tied into The 8 Disciplines as well, making these two problem solving approaches and Scrum feel like a large party where everyone like-minded is invited.

The 5 Whys are pretty straightforward, so we will not linger too much on them. They are, however, absolutely crucial when it comes to pretty much any problem solving process you may want to implement, be it a bug that needs to be fixed or a complex question regarding your future marketing campaign.

The 5 Whys is a problem solving technique nearly 90 years old and which has been developed by the founder of the Toyota company for the first time. Although developed in the 1930s, the method only took to popularity 40 years later, at Toyota. The method is almost religiously followed, though, precisely because it helps teams reiterate essential questions in their problem solving processes.

The 5 Whys stand for an apparently simplistic way of solving issues, but since grand corporations are using it on a daily basis, it is safe to say that this method is legit and that it can provide you with valuable information.

Put simply, what The 5 Whys implies is repeating the question "Why" five times, to get to the root cause of a problem. You can apply the more generalized 5Ws approach (as shown in the sub-chapter explaining The 8 D's) but if you want to make it extremely simple, you can simply ask yourself, and your team, *why*.

Take, for example, a broken computer. If you ask yourself *why* five times in a row, you will eventually get to the final answer, as follows:

1. Why is the computer not functioning? -> It doesn't start up.
2. Why doesn't it start up? -> The motherboard is broken.
3. Why is the motherboard broken? -> A connector has been torn from it.
4. Why is was the connector torn from it? -> The IT manager of the company rushed when he was cleaning the inside of the laptop.
5. Why has he rushed? -> He had several issues to solve on that day and wanted to make sure he gets this out of the way.

The conclusion to this example is that the company either needs an extra IT person to handle this kind of tasks *or* that the current one has to be assigned only with tasks he can handle (both from a quality standpoint and from a quantity one).

When running a 5 Why analysis, you can use two main techniques:

1. The fishbone technique. Also developed at Toyota, the fishbone technique is primarily applied in manufacturing industries, but has been adapted to other fields as well.

   There are several ramifications of this technique, but they all rely on creating a diagram that resembles the tail of a fish where each vertical is an element in the following paradigms:

   - The 5 Ms (used in the manufacturing industry): machine, method, material, manpower, measurement. Sometimes, three more elements are added, creating what is referred to as the 8 Ms: mission, management, and maintenance.
   - The 8 Ps (used primarily in marketing): product, place, promotion, price, process, people, physical evidence, and performance.
   - The 4 Ss (used in services): surroundings, suppliers, systems, and skills.

2. A table. This might seem simplistic, but a simple table or spreadsheet will help you analyze all the potential answers to your 5 Whys and determine the root cause of the issue at hand. It is not as visually stimulating as the fishbone technique, but in some cases, it might be the faster and more straightforward method.

When applying these elements to the fishbone diagram and analyzing them against the problem you need to solve, you will eventually come to five conclusions, according to the 5 Whys methodology.

Last, but not least, it is very important to keep certain things in mind when applying the 5 Whys methodology:

1. Work with the right team and include the management in the process
2. Use a whiteboard to write down, as this will stimulate brainstorming
3. Write down the problem at hand so that everyone can look at it
4. Make sure you and the team make a distinction between causes and symptoms
5. Always keep cause-and-effect in mind
6. Reverse engineer your findings to make sure the root cause you have spotted leads to the same problem you are analyzing and trying to fix
7. Be specific with the answers, ambiguity does not help much
8. Look for the cause with every step along the way and don't jump to direct conclusions
9. Only base all the statements on facts and actual knowledge, rather than assumptions and hunches
10. Look at the problem itself and the process, not the people behind them

11. Things such as human error or a particular person should never be considered as the root cause - it is completely unproductive

12. Encourage everyone to be honest

13. If 5 Whys are not enough, ask yourselves *why* as many times as possible to determine the actual root cause of the problem (the cause which, when eliminated, will help you make sure the problem is not repeated)

14. When you have a final answer, make sure you put it from the point of view of the end customer.

Alright, and how does this tie into Scrum project management?

In terms of mindset, the 5 Whys and Scrum are extremely similar; they are both about the granularity of a problem, respectively of a project. Therefore, they can be reconciled without issue when a problem might arise in the development of a project.

Both the 8 D's and the 5 Whys are problem solving methodologies that connect to Scrum project management and help it be more efficient for everyone: for your team, for you as the delivery agent, for your upper management, and for the client alike.

Chapter Six

The Multiple and Varied Uses of Scrum

As it was mentioned before, Scrum project management is mostly used in software development and the IT industry.

However, it can be applied to pretty much every other industry out there, and this chapter is dedicated to showing you how this can be done and, most importantly *why*.

Scrum brings genuine value wherever it may be applied, and sometimes, even scraps and pieces of the Scrum approach can provide you with a series of benefits. It is always recommended to embrace Scrum fully but in some situations, borrowing concepts like the Daily Scrum or the way the backlog is understood can help you move forward with your projects.

Scrum in the Educational System

It might feel completely odd to start off with a field that is so different than software development, and one that is not even an industry per se.

However, when applied to the educational system, Scrum can be a real game changer, both on the end of the teachers and on the end of the students.

One of the major accomplishments of Scrum in the software industry is the fact that it helps move the projects forward, one step at a time, and it helps the Scrum Master coordinate the tasks and ensure they are delivered on time, on budget, and meeting all the quality requirements of the client.

In the educational system, applying this project management approach can actually bring along the same range of benefits: students will be able to acquire more information and teachers will be able to closely monitor their progress and make amendments or provide further information where they are needed.

Furthermore, the Scrum approach will provide students with a smoother bridge between the educational system and the "real world", as it will make them more accountable and more prepared to deal with various management systems once they get off the school ranks and enter the workforce.

Last, but not least, Scrum helps students build a mentality that's based not on grades and scores, but on accomplishing their goals. Regardless of what these students might decide to do after school, their mindset will be shaped in a way that allows them to *make things happen*, rather than receive instant gratification for every single step they make in their career.

It is important to note that due to school curricula and a variety of standardizations, the deployment of Scrum in a school might be more similar to that of the deployment of this project management methodology in a line management or even Waterfall environment.

However, even when Scrum is used for key classes that shape the students into adults, it can still be extremely beneficial. Even more, implementing Scrum at the teaching level, among the different teachers of a department, can also help them plan their lessons better and provide more information in the given amount of time.

Same as with companies that have been working on a stricter or more traditional project management method until now, deploying Scrum in a school might be met with skepticism. Both teachers who are not familiar with the methodology and students who might feel that they are to be held accountable for too many micro-tasks might feel that the promises of Scrum are nothing but empty air. Therefore, you should be prepared to meet a certain level of resistance from these people.

Let's start with the deployment of Scrum at a higher level in the educational system: the administrative offices. Running any kind of educational program requires strong focus and an inclination towards achieving great results, and this is precisely why Scrum can fit very well in this paradigm.

For instance, having daily meetings with all the stakeholders in an administrative office of a school or an entire district can help them keep up the pace and constantly deliver their "tasks". Some of these might be smaller tasks, such as ensuring all classes are equipped with markers for the whiteboards. Other might be bigger tasks, such as ensuring the sports championships between the schools are well-planned. Each of these major scopes can fit into a Scrum Theme and split into Sprints, according to the needs of the administrative office implementing Scrum in their daily operations.

At a departmental level, Scrum can help the teachers plan their lessons well. When they stop thinking of a semester in terms of a succession of weeks and months and start approaching it with Scrum in mind, they will realize that they can better organize all the information they have to deliver to students. One Sprint can be consisted of three school weeks and it can include a major chapter in the curricula, for example. And every task on the daily list can be a piece of information or sub-topic the teacher needs to approach in class.

At the student level, Scrum can help them become accountable, responsible adults. However, the implementation of a Daily Scrum might feel a bit more difficult in every class and this is where Scrum stops to be a viable option throughout the entire curricula. However, you can still implement Scrum in classes focused on personal development, with the tasks of the students representing a task they have to accomplish to graduate, to get to college, or to acquire a series of skills necessary for their future careers.

In the educational system, Scrum can work as an alternate version of standard practice, one that simply takes the rigidities of the current educational curricula and splits it into smaller tasks. Scrum can provide clarity to all the parties involved in the educational system, from the meal planners to the students themselves.

Scrum and the Service Industry

The service industry can fit very well into the Scrum paradigm, precisely because at its very core, software development too pertains to the same general "Services" industry.

In this field, Scrum can be implemented almost to the letter, boosting productivity, accountability, and the efficiency of every task. Furthermore, because Scrum naturally boosts the tempo of a project's deliverables, it also pushes the entire team to deliver early, to deliver according to the highest standards of quality, and to do all of this while still adhering to a budget that will make the service business profitable.

To understand how Scrum fits into the Service industry, you should first understand how the economy as a whole works. In most cases, the economy of the world is split into three main categories: the primary industries (such as the ones providing the raw materials, including agriculture, for example), the secondary industry (such as those providing products derived from the aforementioned raw materials), and the tertiary industry (such as those providing services that help businesses in the primary, secondary, and even tertiary industry interact better).

Services fall in this category and the more developed a country is, the more likely it is that it will focus more on services than any other type of business.

No matter where in the Service industry you might find yourself, you will learn that your actions and the actions of your team can affect more than just an abstract deliverable: it can affect actual lives. If you work in Finance, your decisions and the way you run a project will affect people's money. If you work in public utilities, your actions will affect the quality of your customers' life.

Being able to deliver fast and with high quality in mind is extremely important regardless of what specific industry you may be working in. And this is precisely where Scrum project management comes into play, helping you move tasks through the backlog and get them done.

One of the particularities of implementing Scrum as a project management method in the Service industry is connected to the fact that in this field of expertise, there are no client requirements per se. Nobody files an order with specific requirements on how they would like to connect to the electricity network; you will have to determine these requirements yourself, based on different studies and surveys.

Once you have gathered some answers from your customers, you will have to use an entity to define them and this entity is quite frequently called "the voice of the customer". Based on what the customer wants, you should create a backlog that works into the requirements you have identified, and you should categorize them specifically.

Furthermore, Scrum can also be implemented in the way you capture the aforementioned voice of the client, as it fits very well into the nature of this type of assignment.

Scrum and the Health Industry

Scrum is the kind of project management approach that is really malleable, and can fit into some of the strictest industries on Earth, including the health industry.

You may not be able to apply Scrum on surgeries or in the emergency rooms, as it would be completely inappropriate and out of the landscape there.

However, there are at least two areas of the health industry where Scrum can make a lot of sense.

One of them, and perhaps the easiest to deploy Scrum to, is hospital management. Same as in the educational system example, Scrum can help hospital managers achieve more in a smaller amount of time and plan better for future actions as well.

Maybe even more importantly than that, Scrum can help hospital management bring cross-functional teams together. When nurses, doctors, and physicians understand each other's tasks and responsibilities, they can better coordinate in the delivery of better health services in a seamless, fast, and efficient way.

In this kind of situation, Scrum brings value that goes beyond anything financial, as it helps building cohesive and self-reliant teams able to save lives in a faster-paced tempo, without compromising on the quality of their services.

Chapter Seven

Bring Your Scrum to the Next Level with Soft Skills and the Right Mindset

You can be the best project manager in the world and hold the most elevate theories on how project management should be done according to your chosen methodology, be it Waterfall, Six Sigma, Scrum, or anything else. But if you do not hold the soft skills and the right mindset, your team will hold you as a tyrant enslaved to rules and conditions, rather than a leader which is what you should be first and foremost.

Soft skills and the right mindset are crucial across all industries and all parallels, for all groups of employees and all generations you may work with but they become increasingly important in software development (where, as mentioned, workforce mobility has grown to be an issue all across the globe) and when working with Millennials.

Let me expand a little on this, to help you understand that soft skills and the right mindset are not just mere "fluffs", but quintessential elements all good project managers should acquire and even more so in Scrum project management, where being self-reliant, honest, and self-managed lies at the very foundation of why and how this methodology works.

Let's start with the value of workforce stability, or tenure, if you want to call it like that.

Tenure is a very important factor in every company, as it can affect a multitude of aspects, including but not limited to the following:

- Productivity. It is a general myth that employees who are older with the company tend to be less productive. In reality, novice employees are much less productive. The reason this happens is because novice employees take more time to learn the ropes of a company, and to get accustomed to their specific role there, to the team, to the management, and even potentially to the management style. Thus, they might work at their lowest productivity for months before they pick up the pace. Tenured employees are, however, more accustomed with the way in which projects are worked on and delivered. With the use of Scrum, new employees can actually reach their maximum efficiency in a short amount of time.

- Trust and cooperation. Even the most sociable person will work better with people he/she already knows and is familiar with and that's a fact I am sure you have tested on your own skin as well. The more cohesive a team is, the stronger the relationships between them are, and the more productive they are.

- Experience. You can bring in the most senior development professionals in your team but if you keep on changing them, you will most likely not help your team reach its maximum potential. Organizational experience is valuable because it will help different team members find solutions faster and solutions that fit your company and your clients, for that matter. Past experiences they have had with a given client, or with a given situation that is particular to your business can be more valuable than experiences that have nothing to do with your company specifically.

Working with Millennials is another reason soft skills and a fair, result-focused mindset are important. This can turn into a long discussion and into a book of its own, but the essentials you need to remember are the following:

- Millennials make up for roughly half of the entire workforce and their numbers will continue to grow as generation X is slowly approaching retirement age. [2]

- Millennials are defined in many ways, but the generally accepted definition is that of "anyone who was born between the 80s and early 2000s". Basically, anyone who was a tween or a teenager at the turn of the Millennia can be considered a Millennial from a generational standpoint.

- In 2018, nearly one quarter of Millennials changed their jobs in the previous year. [3] That's more than any other generation at any given time.

- Millennials need and want to be engaged by their employers, but most frequently this is not related to the money they get, or to other traditional incentives. Millennials are a generation that needs to feel part of something "bigger"; they need to be involved, they need to be part of the story, and part of the success at the same time.

Scrum project management might not be able to control the way Millennials think, their upbringing, or their life goals. What it can do, however, is get your Millennial team members in the right mindset and provide them with the framework of feeling truly included in the success of a project, of being truly heard, and of being part of the team in the truest sense of the word.

Obviously, Millennials are not the only ones who will benefit from Scrum project management, and the IT industry (or any other industry

---

[2] Millennial Insights for the 2020 Labor Market. (2019). Retrieved from http://www.mrinetwork.com/articles/industry-articles/millennial-insights-for-the-2020-labor-market/

[3] Emmons, M. (2019).Key Statistics about Millennials in the Workplace | Dynamic Signal. Retrieved from https://dynamicsignal.com/2018/10/09/key-statistics-millennials-in-the-workplace/

facing tenure issues) will not be the only one to take advantage of this project management method either.

Scrum is universal in its nature. It is Stoic at its very core, drawing its roots from the sincerity of actions and to the determination of the Ancient Romans. Yet, it somehow manages to be very modern as well, adapting to the currently changing landscape of workforce mobility, growing and novice industries, and to the latest technology in management a too.

Create a Good Ambiance

When was the last time you loved going into an office filled with people who hate being there?

Never, most likely.

Truth be told, the corporate world of the 80s and 90s was filled with empty-souled, gray cubicles that only made employees feel more miserable about their condition.

How can you be passionate about your work and stay true to your own self, your own capacity, and your own knowledge when you hate even the actual desk you work on, when your chair makes you sit in an uncomfortable and unhealthy position 8 hours a day, and when your peers only think of resignation the minute they walk into the office?

Even if you start off working passionately in this kind of environment, you will soon end up in the same great pot as everyone else: miserable, full of resent, and lacking productivity.

The IT industry understood this better than anyone, sooner than anyone.

For instance, when Microsoft was first starting off as a significant player on the IT market, employees were allowed to come to work dressed however they pleased. Even more, Gates' management style always included debate and allowed employees to grow every day, encouraging them to attain new skills and be passionate about their work.

Facebook, a far more recent example, is one of the leading tech companies in the world and they too have created an environment of productivity and growth too. One of the techniques they are said to include in their management is encouraging employees to spend a night at the office working not on Facebook's newest features, but on personal projects, together with other team members.

This helps them stay loyal to the company and it helps them stay passionate about their jobs as well.

Again, an entire book could be written on how different IT companies and others keep their employees engaged, even when they are, yes, Millennials. However, this chapter will focus on the basics of how you can do that for your own business through the prism of the Scrum project management approach.

Acknowledging the Power of the Team

Scrum project management is all about the team; that's why the meetings are so important. The guy ensuring the quality of the Facebook schedule feature in your social media management software development project might not be that involved in the design of the logo of the new software that was handled by the new girl. But even so, the fact that they are both brought together in the same meeting, on a daily basis, will make them feel like they actually belong to the team and that, no matter how large or small, simple or complex their tasks may be, they are still important.

The Daily Standups meet a series of goals in Scrum project management. On the one hand, they allow the Scrum Master to accurately assess and plan the situation of the Sprint. On the other hand, they help the team members correctly assess and plan their own situation and take corrective action if necessary.

In Scrum management, each member of the team is there for a purpose, is part of the story, and helps moving the project forward with their skills. The team is the central and indivisible "secret ingredient" of the entire operation and each team member works as an indispensable cell in the wider network of team members, tasks, Sprints, and Themes.

Without a correct understanding of the team and its true value, there cannot be true Scrum project management. And, in the end, there cannot be real progress in the development of the project either. Thus, it's important for everyone engaged to acknowledge the value of the team.

Without the team as the central concept connecting all the elements of Scrum project management, you are just dealing with a bunch of individuals who randomly meet every morning, at the same time, to absurdly answer the same three questions in a given number of minutes.

Acknowledging the Power of the Individual

The accomplishments of the team as a whole are always more important in Scrum project management than the accomplishments of the single individual; however this isn't because individuals are not important (not in any way, actually). In the Scrum mindset, each team member is part of the mechanization that transforms a theorized project into reality and deliverability.

Compare this to the natural ecosystem, perhaps the greatest project ever created and delivered. If heat didn't evaporate the water in lakes, oceans, and rivers, rain wouldn't exist. If rain didn't exist, plants wouldn't exist, vegetarian beings wouldn't exist, omnivorous beings wouldn't exist, and, in consequence, mankind would not exist either.

And this is just one small example (the equivalent of a Sprint, if you may). Our entire existence on Earth is dependent on a multitude of elements coming together to create the "whole package": a livable planet.

Take any of these elements out of the picture and you are destroying an entire chain of cause and effect, eventually altering our very possibility of living on the third rock from the sun.

The same goes in project management through the Scrum perspective as well. If you take any of the team members out of the ecosystem you have worked hard to create, you will disrupt the flow of the work and the cadence of each Sprint. Eventually, the project as a whole would cease to exist, or it would exist in a form that may not be satisfactory for the end customer.

I am more than certain your team will feel proud when their hard work is acknowledged especially publicly. But truly, nothing can actually compare to a warm individual "Thank You". It is wired into our very neural network: a simple phrase of gratitude can push us further and give us energy to continue our work.

And if you need yet another reason to give thanks, well, learn that it can make *you* happier too. According to a Harvard study, thanking and showing gratitude can make you happier.

Even more, Harvard studies also point out to the fact that showing gratitude can actually make you feel more optimistic (as opposed to showing irritation, which can lead to more pessimism). [4]

That is precisely why the Daily Standup doesn't start with the road blockers, but with the tasks that were accomplished on the previous day: it gives people a sense of optimism that they *did* accomplish something and this changes their mindset about the day ahead as well, no matter how difficult the upcoming tasks may be.

Thanking your team at an individual and at a collective level is only the polite and humane way to treat things. Same as you, the people

---

[4] Publishing, H. (2019). Giving thanks can make you happier - Harvard Health. Retrieved from https://www.health.harvard.edu/healthbeat/giving-thanks-can-make-you-happier

working for the deliverables of your project are *human*, and they are bound to react positively when positive thoughts are bestowed on them.

Sounds poetic and it might sound like it has zero points of connection to Scrum as an Agile project management methodology, but it can make all the difference in the world, drawing the line between constantly asking the team what they are working on and actually treating them as a valuable asset to the project and the company.

Acknowledging the Power of the Physical Environment

Remember the example with the gray, cubicle office that dehumanized the work experience and drained passion out of employees, instead of instilling it in them?

These days, it comes almost without saying that most IT companies have some sort of game or recreation room on their premises, that people can work remotely on a recurrent basis or simply when they need to, and that offices need to look nice. These concepts have been borrowed into pretty much every other industry on Earth, and most Human Resource and business professionals acknowledge that a nice-looking, welcoming office is not about the aesthetics and image of the company only, but about the productivity of its employees as well.

Studies show that the work place environment can affect the work of the employees[5] on multiple grounds - including, but not limited to:

- Performance and productivity
- Creativity
- Collaboration and communication
- Overall satisfaction

---

[5] THE IMPACT OF THE PHYSICAL WORK ENVIRONMENT ON ORGANIZATIONAL OUTCOMES: A STRUCTURED REVIEW OF THE LITERATURE. (2019). Retrieved from https://jfmer.org/doi/full/10.22361/jfmer/76637

Creating a suitable work environment for your employees is about a variety of factors, such as:

- The space they have
- The spatiality
- The colors used in the office
- The comfort (good chairs, the ability to increase and reduce temperature at will)
- The overall vibe of the decor
- The lighting
- The existence of a play room or recreation room

And the list goes on.

Basically, your work environment should be as pleasant as possible, and it makes all the sense in the world to be so, given that both you and your team spend nearly more than one third of your lives there for as many years as you are active on the workforce.

To put that in perspective, you sleep for one third of your life (provided that you sleep the mandatory 8-hours-a-night) and you live outside of the office for the other third of life. Thus, spending 8 hours in a gloomy or uncomfortable environment will naturally lead to a lot of frustration and remorse.

Those are emotions you truly don't want in your team regardless of whether you use Scrum to manage it or not. In Scrum, it is even more important to make sure your team members are OK with everything around them; because these are such tight-knit teams, both optimism and pessimism, both satisfaction and dissatisfaction, and both pleasant experiences and unpleasant can spread out rapidly to all the members of the team.

You literally cannot afford *one* unhappy team member because accepting that would mean that soon enough, the person sitting next to him will face the same level of dissatisfaction, and the person he hangs out with at lunch will feel it too, and then before you know it, even the intern will feel the same negative emotions even though everyone was extremely excited just a Sprint or two ago.

Aside from everything I have mentioned here, there are also some physical workplace elements that will help you build a better and more cohesive Scrum team:

- White boards. Although computers and software can be used for the Daily Scrums and the other meetings, having a white board in the room will help your team stay focused on the tasks at hand because they will have all the actions right there, in front of their eyes, for the entire day.

- Light. This is more of a preference in some teams, but you should provide the members with the possibility to adjust the level of natural light that comes into the room, and the temperature of artificial light.

- Open space. An open workspace brings the entire team together, but separates the different micro-teams through partitions.

- Enough space to walk through the chairs and desks without difficulty.

- A discussion table where team members can gather to brainstorm and discuss issues.

- Meeting rooms with projectors, white boards, and all the equipment needed for a seamless, fast, and efficient meeting, be it a daily one or a Sprint review.

- Areas where team members can think in silence.

- Areas where team members can make personal phone calls.

- Sound isolation from the other teams of the company that might be noisier (i.e. the customer service department who talks on the phone all day).

Acknowledging the Power of the Tools

This is not about project management tools per se, but about the tools of the trade your team members will need to perform at their very best.

This includes both hardware and software as well.

For instance, you wouldn't provide your designer with a 10-year-old computer because they wouldn't be able to run the latest image editing and design software on it.

Likewise, you wouldn't provide them with an old version of an image editing software because it will prevent them from achieving the best looking and most modern results.

The same applies to software too. For instance, you wouldn't ask the accountants in a company to simply use a free version of a sheet editing software just to save money on the licenses; so why should your developers work on outdated and potentially free software?

Aside from providing the team with the bare necessities to do their work, it would also be very nice for you to offer them their choice of equipment. So, if one person loves working on an Apple computer and would need a soundproof pair of headphones to isolate themselves from the exterior sounds when doing something that requires all their focus, you should definitely consider providing it to them. It will create a sense of loyalty, it will show that person he/she is important for the company, and it will help them stay more productive and efficient.

Acknowledging the Power of Identification

Even the most individualist and anti-social person on Earth still feels the need to belong to a group even if that is the group of the individualists and anti-socials. We are wired that way: ever since our beginning on this planet, we have worked in groups. This trait stays embedded in our genes and pushes us to dreaming of a sense of identity.

Some identify with the nation they come from, others identify with the music they listen to but to some extent at least, most of us yearn for this rather ambiguous and definitely abstract concept we call "identity".

It's in the basic pyramid of needs elaborated by Maslow, right there, in the upper range; meaning that, if the primary needs are fulfilled, people will always search for a sense of belonging.

Providing your team members with that at work is a good idea. The more connected one is to the tribe, the more likely it is that one will stay true to the goals of the tribe and to their role in it.

There are several ways you can do this. You can adopt a mascot for your Scrum team, you can get a pet everyone takes care of by turn, or you can simply embrace a certain flag, a certain name, or a certain color.

Furthermore, you should constantly encourage your team and you should always make them feel like their principles and ideals are the same as those of the team, and the other way around. This should function similarly to how some people identify with the values of the country they come from (e.g. America is the country upon a hill everyone should be looking up to, and thus, patriotic Americans work towards that goal).

Bringing your team together is about so much more than just bringing them in the same physical space. It is about the entire experience you create for them: the sense of importance at a team and individual level, the sense of belonging, the sense of "feeling like home" when they walk into the office and take a seat at their preferred desk or on their favorite beanie bag, and so on. More than anything, it is about making your team members feel that they can adhere to the same set of high values of Scrum management: trust, honesty, self-reliance, and personal and team growth.

Chapter Eight

The Skills of a Great Scrum Master

A great team does not just happen; as it was shown in the previous sections, it takes quite a lot of hard work and determination to build the kind of Scrum team that fully identifies with the values of the Scrum project management philosophy in general.

And for all that to happen, the experience of a great Scrum Master is needed to steer the team in the right direction.

Of course, understanding how Scrum works and what the main techniques behind it will help you apply Scrum to virtually every industry under the sun, as it was also shown in a previous chapter.

Beyond that, however, you need to possess a series of skills that will help you instill the Scrum project management approach into your team members, because a great project manager leads not by tossing around rules and techniques, but by living up to his/ her own examples.

You wouldn't necessarily say that if you saw a Scrum Master job ad, whether it's a not so inspiring one or an inspired) one. However, this is a job requirement that lies in the very nature of the Scrum project management approach. It may not be included in most job descriptions, but it's right there, between the lines, transpiring through the actual job requirements and into the daily mindset of a Scrum Master.

So, how do you get there if you are relatively new to Scrum project management?

There are a lot of actions you can take in that direction, but if we had to narrow it down to the very basics, it would be all about fourteen basic elements you should consider. All of these will be discussed further on in the remainder of this chapter's section dedicated to Scrum Master skills.

Mastery of Scrum Beyond the Rules

As I was saying above, being a great Scrum Master is not solely about the rules and regulations of the system, but about much more than that.

Compare it to martial arts, similarly to how the Six Sigma approach does. A truly talented martial arts master knows all the insides of the martial arts he/she is representing. However, it takes a true talent to go beyond that and transcend the rules into the very granular philosophy of what martial arts are - and what a specific branch of this Eastern self-defense spectrum encompasses as well.

The Scrum Master is a servant of the company, of the project, of the client requirements and, at a meta level, of the Scrum methodology *and* they are a leader in it. Circling back to the martial arts example above, the master does not make the rules of the martial art he/ she represents, but follows them as a true servant of what they mean. At the same time, he/she is able to instill more than a deep knowledge of these rules into the people who follow his/her teachings in class.

This entire concept might feel like a complete contradiction - but it lies at the very philosophical foundation of what Scrum is truly all about.

How do you reconcile the contradictory terms, "leader" and "servant"? By doing these things:

1. **You lead without being authoritative.** It is a well-known fact already that being too authoritative will eventually lead to people resenting, and even resigning from, the company and you, as its management representative. It is said, jokingly, that people do not quit companies per se, but that they quit their bosses. This

can happen for a variety of reasons, but one of the most common ones is wrongly inputted authority.

A true Scrum Master leads by example, by kindness, by the kind of fatherly or motherly authority that is both candid and well set in stone. If you ever had a figure of authority in your life that you respected and loved (a grandfather, perhaps), and whose words you always perceived as letters of the law, think of them when picturing your main project management goal.

2. **Leave aside your ego.** As I was also iterating this before, there is no *I* in a Scrum team; truly, there should be no I in any kind of team, as the saying goes - but with the Scrum approach, this becomes monumentally important for the success of the entire methodology.

As a Scrum Master, you need to let go of your own vanity and ego. Admit when you are wrong and set an example by doing this out loud, in front of your entire team. Accept opinions. Let go of anything your own self could impose on the team members, regardless of whether it is related to how you see work ethics or how you think one should behave in and out of the office.

Your ego will only impede you from achieving the great things you can achieve through Scrum project management, so leave it at the door when you step into the office, together with any kind of personal problem you might have.

3. **Always act fairly towards all the members of your team.** It would be a lie to say that you will never have "favorites". Even as a parent, you might still be more inclined to love a child just a touch more, for a wide range of reasons. Sure, it's not ethical, and it's not recommended by anyone who has ever studied child psychology, but it happens frequently.

The difference between having a favorite and acting on your preference is precisely where you should set your focus. It is one thing to like a team member more than the other because they work better, because they are funnier, or because they instill in their workmates the kind of energy you really need on a daily basis.

It is a completely different thing, however, to act on this and set that person above anyone else. You would be no different than an old-school teacher who likes the class nerd more and gives them better grades even when they do not necessarily deserve it.

Act fairly towards the members of your team. This means accepting that even the brilliant ones can make mistakes and even those who do not necessarily perform outstandingly can sometimes surprise you in the best of ways.

Even more, act fairly towards those who are honest by fixing faulty elements of the team mechanisms. Yes, that might sometimes be a faulty team member, and other times, it may simply be a poorly planned Sprint.

4. **Be self-confident.** If you want people to believe in you, you first need to believe in yourself, and you need to emanate that through every pore. A Scrum Master (or any other kind of project manager) that fumbles and stumbles when it comes to decision making is a weak manager, one that does not instill confidence in the team, and one that can eventually lead to the dissolution of the team itself.

We're only human, so it's natural to have your own insecurities and demons to fight with. However, when you step into the Scrum Master cloak, you need to fake it; and yes, you need to do this " 'till you make it" as well.

5. **Be humble.** The more arrogant you are, the worse your image will be in the eyes of each and every team member. It's one thing to be self-confident, and it's a completely different one to be arrogant, so accept humbleness as one of your main guidelines and points of moral compass. Accept that you can make

mistakes, accept that you are not the King or Queen of the Hill, and do all of this knowing full-heartedly that you are leading people in the good direction.

Sounds, again, like a paradox, but more than anything, it is all about *balance*.

6. **Be open to discussion and approachable.** This is tightly connected into the idea of humbleness and self-confidence because a person who is self-confident is not afraid to be approached, and a person who is not arrogant will make it easy for people to approach him/her.

Why is approachability and openness so important in Scrum? Because you need to make sure your team members trust you entirely - even when they might have a problem they want to discuss with you in private, rather than in one of the meetings.

Keep your door open in a figurative sense (figurative because you will most likely share the same open space with your team) and keep your mind, your eyes, and your soul open as well.

7. **When changes must be implemented, instill a lack of fear in your team members.** Let's face it: most humans are not created to love change. You might love a change of hairstyle or even a change of car, but even so, changing drastic elements of your life is not in your nature or anyone else's for that matter.

There is a very good reason people started to settle down to being farmers all those hundreds of thousands of years ago: change was not in their nature either.

We are one of the most resilient and adaptable species on Earth, and change has been wired into our DNA the same way our teeth have. Yet, this doesn't make change a pleasant experience.

Acknowledging the fact that change is scary is wisdom. Knowing that you should not in any way share that fear with your team is true Scrum Master wisdom. The least minor a change is presented to be, the less people will be inclined to think it will be a bad experience.

Present changes through an optimistic perspective, at all times. Dress it up in the latest fashion and the sparkliest accessories, even if, underneath it all, it might look more like a Gremlin monster than a Furby. Doing this will give your team a sense of confidence and optimism, as opposed to not doing it, which will give them a sense of fear, unproductivity, and maybe even the sudden need to sign their resignation.

8. **Adopt a diplomatic approach, but make sure you don't make yourself look like a stereotypical politician.** Whenever in discussions with your team members, be sure to be diplomatic and present problems just the way an embassy emissary would: with tact and delicacy.

At the same time, be sure this doesn't make you look like a scheming politician who knows the "truth" but hides it from the world for his/ her own benefit.

It's a fragile balance to reach, but once there, you will be more respected and you will instill the same kind of ethic in your team. So, when they will have to feedback each other, they will do it just as gracefully as you did it.

9. **Be transparent in your communication.** Scrum Management is not about the big wooden words and the constructed messages. It is transparent down to its very core; just think of the nature of the Daily Standups, for example.

The way you communicate and the frequency of your communication should be transparent as well. Don't hide behind your small finger; say things are they are, but do it in a polite and nicely-wrapped way.

10. **Be selfless.** This is tied into the whole "leaving your ego at the door" concept, but brings the ball in your own court. Being selfless means spending the extra hours at the office to make sure

the next Sprints are well planned and none of the team members are over-tasked. It means budgeting great laptops for everyone else first, and only then factoring yourself into the equation.

It means being anything but selfish in terms of everything connected to how you work, where you do it, and with whom. Your team comes first in all situations, because they are the ones who will eventually deliver the final product.

11. **Guide and protect, but don't be "too much" for your team.** In many examples, the Scrum Master is portrayed as a shepherd who steers the team in the right direction. Do keep in mind that this does not imply the idea that your team is mindless and needs constant guidance, though.

    Look at it in military terms, rather than sheepherding ones. Your team members rely on you to point them in the best direction, but they don't want to be overly protected. They don't want to feel like that kid in school who was constantly hand-held by his mom all the way to the school doors.

12. **Stay in tune with the technical knowledge, if necessary.** Some might be under the impression that a Scrum Master needs to have the in-depth technical knowledge of the team he/she is leading. However, that is not necessary. In fact, it is quite unproductive, because it will eventually make you feel like you have to jump in and help with tasks hands-on, rather than stay away from them and remain an objective outsider.

    While it may not be important, and sometimes not even recommended, to be a tech ace as a Scrum Master, it is still important that you are familiar with the concepts and that you are fully in the loop with whatever your team members are working on.

13. **Accept that your job is never fully done.** As a Scrum Master, you never get to say "yes, I am completely done with this" even

when the deliverable is done and when it has already reached the hands of the client.

They may or may not come back with feedback but your job is still not done once the feedback is implemented, as they may always come back for additions and revisions that occurred due to a change in strategy, a change in technology, or simply a change in trends.

You never get to fully put a project to bed, as long as you stick with a company, of course.

14. **Be an inspiration.** Being a Scrum Master is all about giving your team an example of how they should perceive their work and their daily tasks.

    Be an inspiration to your team and they will thank you for it, maybe not now, and maybe not even in two years from now, but sooner or later, they will look back at that Scrum Manager who taught them how to be honest with themselves.

Scrum Management is more than project management methodology; it is a life philosophy that applies into your work and expands into your personal life. Even if you are not necessarily a Scrum Master, applying the aforementioned principles to your day to day life is the healthiest and most balanced thing you can do for yourself in a world that has lost its patience, its time, and its ability to be fully sincere.

Chapter Nine

The Shining Skills of a Scrum Team

Scrum management cannot exist outside of the realms of the Team as the most important cell of the entire planning process.

Of course, as a Scrum Master, you need to meet certain criteria and apply certain skills in your life, as a project manager and as an individual.

What about your team, though, what are the skills they should acquire as a single organism?

Well, it all starts with the attitude or what we would call the mindset, in the paradigm of this book.

If your team starts with a negative attitude, and if they don't believe in the power of Scrum (as religiously fanatic as this might sound), you will not be able to change their mind forcefully. All you can do is change their mind through the power of example; showing them that, for instance, a deliverable happened earlier precisely because they were all open minded enough to adopt something new and maybe extremely different than what they were they were used to.

In most situations, the attitude of a team member is far more important and crucial than the skill. Don't get this wrong: it is of the utmost importance that you bring people in your team who can actually provide quality and expertise for the entire project.

However, even the most talented team member can be a bad seed if their attitude is not congruent with the values you and your team believe in. One bad apple can lead, as I was mentioning earlier, to a series of unfortunate events that might even culminate with the dissolution of the team in the current formula.

Going for the Jedi, Guru, Rockstar and Ninja

If you have been on any job board in the last few years, you have probably seen at least a good dozen of job announcements advertising positions for development ninjas, QA gurus, and rockstar designers.

Indeed, the current is slowly dying out, and for good reasons too, as it was growing to be much too overused.

Beyond that, the underlying motivation behind these job announcements is that everyone seems to be searching for the next Bill Gates and Paul Allen duo, all rolled in one.

Again, don't get us wrong, talent is important, but in Scrum, the arrogant attitude associated with gurus, ninjas, and other similar denominations can be actually damaging for the entire team. When one element sees themselves higher in the ranks than everyone else, it can be felt in everyday activities, from the way they deliver the Daily Standup to the way they treat people who are more junior than them.

This is a completely hurtful attitude towards any kind of team, and much less in a Scrum team, where the congruence, compatibility, and cohesiveness of the team as the nuclei of the entire project lies at the very basis of the Scrum philosophy.

So, should you go for the talented Jedi, or for someone who can deliver great work and continue to grow?

Definitely for the latter. As mentioned before, going for the Jedi can damage the structure and the energies in your entire team. At the same time, hiring someone who might not have a halo of superstardom to them, but is a good team player, who is modest and humble without lacking self-confidence, and who is keen on growing will actually make your team more "whole" and it will complement the missing elements.

Adherence to Scrum Values

Even if the person you are adding to your team is not fully familiar with Scrum and the values that define it, it is still very important to look for someone with a personality and psychological profile that will fit into the Scrum paradigm.

I will not lie: Scrum is not for everyone. More than anything, being a Scrum team member is all about discipline and honesty; the same skills as in martial arts, if you want to go back to that example.

Your team members should possess the qualities that make them great Scrum teams. Sometimes, these are more important than highly advanced knowledge of their craft, precisely because these qualities are bound to push not only them but also their peers towards greater achievements.

Other than discipline, what are some of the other qualities an excellent Scrum team member should possess?

Here we go:

1. **Energy.** Understandably so, we can't all be little furballs of energy and positivity all the time. Even so, the general vibe you should get from your team members is that of growth, and an overall "let's do it" attitude.

    Don't be fooled, though. Sometimes, the friendliest and most humorous people can be utterly deenergizing, particularly during Daily Scrums, where they tend to sap all the energy in the room, unintentionally, most of the times.

    If you see a team member is dragging everyone down in the melancholy box, have a talk to them and see if there is anything you can do to help. Sometimes, it might actually be within your power to change things for them and make their lives better.

2. **Curiosity.** One of the main tenets of a good, functional, and efficient Scrum team is a permanent orientation towards growth.

And in order for that to happen, you want to make sure all of your team members are naturally curious. Their interest within the field of expertise is shown by how they stay up to date with the latest news, how they are permanently searching for solutions, and the general attitude they have towards the new elements.

All of these traits can be fairly easily tested in the recruitment phase.

Beyond that, your team members should also be naturally inclined to learn everything about other topics they interest them. The more hobbies they have, the more curious their minds are, as a general rule of thumb. Yes, a Jack of all Trades is a Master of None, indeed. But if the trades your team members are interested in are diverse and if they show that they have a personality developed outside of the boundaries of their personal field of expertise, it is likely that these people are also growth oriented as well.

3. **Respect.** This is very tightly tied into the idea that your team members should not be arrogant. From the way they say hello to the person taking care of the office cleaning to the way they treat their peers, even if they are on a lower experience scale than them, everything can make a difference.

    A person who shows respect is always more likely to be a person who will be honest in all situations, and whose Daily Standup will be a true reflection of their past and current activities.

4. **Empathy.** No matter where they are situated on their career path, your team members should be empathic.

    This helps with the cohesiveness of the entire team and it helps them easily adhere to the high-level values of the Scrum philosophy in general. Empathy is precisely what will make a team member help another when they seem them struggle, and it is one of the reasons the same team member will choose to be honest, both to others and to themselves, in their activity.

5. **Sociability.** Now, this might be a tricky one, especially if you are a software development Scrum Master, as developers are not necessarily known to be the friendliest people on Earth. This is, of course, a stereotype and a generalization, but all in all, engineers and programmers tend to be more introverted, which does not necessarily mean they will not be empathic or sociable in any way.

   A friendly face who smiles every day when they walk into the office and when they deliver their Daily Scrum keeps the positive energies in the team, making it more likely for all the members to actually like the Scrum approach and genuinely adhere to its values.

These are, of course, just some of the traits your team members should have but they are also the most important ones. Yes, it is highly important that you hire people who are talented and experienced and who will bring professional value into the team. Aside from all that, however, the attitude and the personality of a member can be more important than anything.

Chapter Ten

Implementing Scrum with your Team

If you have read a thing or two about Scrum, you will see a phrase that keeps being reiterated every time someone tries to convince you of the advantages this approach has to offer: it works, and it makes people more efficient.

How do you measure the efficacy of Scrum in your team, though?

Is it all about the deliverables and key performance indicators, or is there something else?

Being able to measure the efficiency of the entire project is extremely important if you want to make sure you can report your results upwards the management stream. Regardless of whether or not the rest of the company uses Scrum or any other management methodology, you will still have to report your results sooner or later, and for that to happen, you need to keep in mind some important metrics.

The Meaningful Metrics to Mind

Before we jump into the actual metrics, it is important to mention that there are two types of metrics in Scrum:

- The good metrics: used to determine where you may be at some point and guide the team towards improvement
- The evil metrics: indicators that show you have been micromanaging a team member's performance, and to show that the morale in your team is low

The main metrics you should follow when running a Scrum project are the following:

1. **Sprint burndown.** This metric is generated at the end of each day, aside from the last day of every Sprint. The way you draw this metric is by calculating the time required to finish all the tasks of a project, and then connecting the total time spent on that current day and the total time spent on the previous day with the necessary time you still need to finish all the tasks in the Sprint.

   Basically, what this metric will show you is whether or not you are on track with the delivery of every Sprint's product and with the delivery of the final product as well. For instance, this metric will help you determine if the task time estimates were correct, if team members took time off (unplanned for), or if any impediments have delayed the project deliverables in any way.

   If your Sprint burndown shows that your team will not achieve their goal for this Sprint, it is important to take action in this sense. The best thing you can do is remove all the impediments in the way of efficient work; but if that doesn't work, you might also want to discuss with the product owner(s) and see if the scope of the project can be re-adjusted.

   Furthermore, if you have determined the failure of the current Sprint has occurred due to an inaccurate time management and estimation, you should definitely implement the acquired knowledge for the planning of the following Sprints.

   Sprint breakdowns are not always bad. Sometimes, they might show that you are ahead of your deliveries in every way, and this is actually good for the team morale and for your reports as well.

2. **Sprint interference.** This metric is all about productivity and calculating the correct capacity planning when interferences appear in your Sprint. The Sprint interference is to be generated during each Sprint planning.

To calculate this metric, calculate the time spent by any of the team members for any of the backlog tasks that are not connected to the Sprint, and then draw a line between these data points.

The Sprint interference will help you determine the time needed to fix any kind of Sprint disruption in the future, basing your new estimates on historical data.

In an ideal world, your backlog would not be disrupted in any way, but there is a long list of issues that might turn your plans upside down (from team members falling sick to technical disruptions). Therefore, it is quite important to be able to plan for this kind of problems as well.

3. **Enhanced release burndown.** This type of metric should be generated at the end of every Sprint. It is an approach only some Scrum Masters embrace, so it's not a general rule of Scrum project management.

   Different theoretical schools of thought in project management have different takes on the Enhanced release burndown, but in most cases, the calculation of this metric is a bit more complex than the calculation of any other metric in Scrum project management.

   More specifically, when you want to determine the Enhanced release burndown, you should start by calculating all the remaining points for the PBIs you see in the product backlog of the *next* release. Connect all these points using a line.

   Further on, look at each Sprint and calculate the sum between the PBI story points that have been added to the backlog *after* the beginning of the project. Connect all these points using a line as well.

   What will result from these steps is a graph where the X-axis is the evolution of a team through the different backlog items and the Y-axis represents the items that have been added post-planning.

What will this help you with?

The graph will help you determine how many sprints are necessary to see the product ready for release; you will see this at the intersection between the X and the Y axes. If these two do not meet, you should reconsider the entire planning because it is quite likely that the product will never be released in full.

4. **Remedial focus.** This metric is all about the quality of the final deliverable and it will help you and your team determine how much time was spent on fixing the bugs to ensure the quality of the final product. The Remedial focus metric should be generated at the end of each Sprint.

To generate it, you will have to calculate the sum of all the product backlog items (including new and unexpected items and bugs). Then, you will have to calculate the sum of the items that were connected to working on bugs and correlate these data points with the first ones.

The Best Characteristics of a Successful Standup

The Daily Standup lies at the foundation of Scrum project management, so it is quintessentially important that you do these meetings the right way. Simply gathering people in a room and asking them what they are up to will not cut it. You need to create an atmosphere that will promote the Daily Standup as a healthy organizational initiative.

The Daily Standup should take place, as the name suggests, every day. You choose the location of this meeting, but keep in mind that it should be easy for all the team members to attend it every day and that it should allow each of them to actually stand up when their turn comes. Furthermore, all team members and the Scrum Master should be able to see each other, so you might need an open space for this. It is not mandatory, of course, but if you want everyone to be comfortable and if you want to make sure nobody misses the point of the entire meeting, this kind of space will surely help.

Why is it so important to stand up, rather than sit? It's all about the psychology behind this type of meetings: by standing up, you feel more accountable for your own actions and you are more likely to keep it short and to the point. Furthermore, the standing up makes the meeting feel livelier and more focused on action, rather than reiterating a plan.

How much time should your standup take?

It is not a very good idea to impose a timing on your team. It might irritate some who will find your timing too restrictive. Instead, discuss this with your team: how much are they ready to invest in this and how much would not be very disruptive?

Furthermore, the exact time for each Daily Scrum should also be established with your team and, if some of your members work remotely, you should take into account potential time zone differences as well.

Once you have established the basics, you should also establish some ground rules everyone has to follow:

- The meeting will start every day at the same hour, no matter of who attends and who is late
- Suggest some sort of "punishment" for those who are late, such as doing three sit-ups or adding a dollar to a jar you will use to buy something for the team at some point.
- Try to organize yourselves in a circle around the task board
- Always answer the three basic questions and do not expand the discussion any further: mention the things you achieved on your previous day of work, what you plan to accomplish today, and what impediments you might have on your road.
- Make sure everyone is talking about their tasks as they are referenced on the task board. This will help everyone understand what item is being discussed, and it will help

everyone keep track of what is on the task board, so that it is always up to date.

- Maintain the energy at a high level. This meeting should jumpstart the day, not make everyone feel drawn into an energyless black hole.

- Always focus on improvement, not just in the sense of problem solving, but in the sense of finding better solutions every day.

- Maintain your focus and the focus of your team. Jokes and giggles are fun, of course, but this meeting should be very succinct and very to the point so try to keep everyone in the game.

- For the Daily Standup to be efficient and fast, it is important that constant communication is maintained among the members of the team that are involved in working on the same item, as well as other parties that might be interested.

- When a team member stands up and describes the status of a task he/she is working on, he/she should mention how the work is progressing, as well as anything else that might be of interest to the team and Scrum Master.

- The information shared by each team member should be directed to the entire team, not just the Scrum Master. If you feel a team member directs their information solely at you, try to take your eyes away from them a little. This is quite important because when you are addressing just the Scrum Master, you make the entire meeting feel like a micromanagement meeting, rather than an energizing one.

- Start on a positive note. Allow everyone a few minutes before each Daily Standup to socialize, joke around, and share personal stories. This helps the team feel better, more energized, and it makes the meeting less of an obligation and more of a pleasure.

Drawing an Adequate Task Board

Aside from the Daily Scrum, the task board is the second most important element of the Scrum philosophy. Having all the tasks in front of your eyes all day long and seeing how they progress helps you stay focused on what matters: getting things done and pushing the project further.

One of the first decisions you will have to make when it comes to creating the task board is whether it should be digital or physical. In general, it is recommended that you go with the physical task board on this, for a series of reasons. One of the most important ones is the way humans work: there is something really satisfying about actually moving a sticky note into the "Done" column.

Even so, it is understandable if you might have to use digital "boards". Some of the most famous project management tools that fit in this category are Trello and Asana, which tap right into the way Scrum works and what it needs. The reason you might have to settle on a digital board instead of a physical one is mostly related to your team members' physical presence in the office. With permanent or recurrent remote work on the rise , digital might actually win the long run.

Another important factor to consider when creating your task board is how you organize the actual sticky notes/ items on it. One of the best ways to do it is by splitting them in four columns: Not Started, In Progress, Verification, and Done.

Furthermore, you should also pay attention to what each item or sticky note on your board contains. You need to make sure it is named properly, but you also want to make sure the information written on it will trigger the correct actions in the team members responsible with dealing with those particular issues.

Conclusion

People are seriously in love with over-complicating everything.

It might be in our nature, but that is doubtful, given how reticent most human beings are in the face of change.

Most likely, our passion for over-complicating concepts and situations is due to a long history of being fed into literature and movies that are all about the intrigue, the complication, the adversity.

True, you would hate Star Wars if there was no Darth Vader or if he was a wimp unable to live up to his bad name. So it is understandable why both literature (high and low brow alike) and Hollywood have been feeding us complicated plots: we like it, and it feeds our imagination.

When it comes to over-complicating things in real life, though, you can only be led astray. Imagination can save you from a lot of bad situations and creativity can help you be better at anything you may do, but adding unnecessary scenarios on top of what you already have will only create chaos and disorder.

Most of the problems you encounter at a professional level and at a personal one are straightforward. Fixing them is not necessarily easy, but it can be broken down into steps you make towards success.

The IT industry understood this earlier and better than anyone. When faced with the propensity of a project that involves hundreds of features and thousands of lines of code, they did not step back, weeping in silence, nor did they start to create entire stories and philosophies around what was standing before them.

They took the bull by its horns and chopped it down to the manageable, easily digestible tasks that would eventually win the race.

The Scrum project management methodology was born in an environment that encourages questioning and debate, that puts the flow and the action above anything else, and that is fast paced in nature. Just to put things in perspective a little and help you understand just how fast paced the IT industry is, imagine that you are now holding in your smartphone more processing power than any other personal computer in the 90s.

This kind of advances would not have been realistic or even reachable if it weren't for the IT industry's "yes, we can" attitude. Constantly pushing the edges of technology further and further does come with a price, though: you will have to leave behind negativity and always focus on doing things, doing them fast, and doing them with quality in mind as well.

The Scrum project management approach is all about speed, reiterations, and not taking on more than you can chew. It's easy to become overwhelmed by the grandeur of a software program and all the work that goes in it; but when everything is split in small bits and pieces that are easy to manage one after the other, everything feels simpler.

Even more importantly, everything moves faster as well.

Scrum encourages growth on all levels and completely eradicates the "I" in the "Team" we have heard so much about. In Scrum, it doesn't matter if your experience is executive level or if you are just starting out: everyone is pushed to go beyond their limits and create something amazing together, as a team.

From the way meetings are done to the soft skills a project manager in Scrum should possess, everything about this project management methodology is about the people and just how efficient and brilliant they can be when the right framework is set for them.

Scrum is simple, it really is. You don't need to be a rocket scientist to understand its basics and you don't need a degree in clinical psychiatry to be able to understand the finesse elements of why Scrum is about the *people*, rather than the *project*.

Same as with everything else under the sun, however, people like to complicate Scrum and make it feel a lot more troublesome and headache-inducing than it actually is. Daily meetings?Colored post its?

Constantly managing your own tasks without being assigned anything? Those are almost preposterous to someone who has been using conventional project management for years or even decades.

For those who understand that the simplicity of Scrum is also what makes it work so well, this project management approach is precisely what they need from a long list of points of view, starting with its ease of use and ending to the fact that in a Scrum team, everyone is responsible for their actions.

All this talk about simplicity might feel as a direct opposition to everything that was mentioned throughout this book, especially given how Scrum was compared to other project management methods. When you look beyond the differences and the challenges of implementing Scrum within other systems, you will soon realize that everything is much easier than it seems and that it follows the kind of infallible logical sequence you need as a project manager dealing with anything.

What I hope this book has achieved is showing you how Scrum works as part of a network: a network of project management approaches and a network of human beings who react to emotional triggers. From the very introduction of the book, I mentioned that it would focus on two large parts: Scrum vs. Everything Else and Scrum vs. Yourself and Your Team.

By this point, I am more than certain that you have deepened your knowledge in the art of Scrum project management and that you are one step closer to becoming a Scrum Master in the fullest sense of the word.

I hope that you have:

- learned why there are so many project management methods
- learned how to spot some of the most important ones
- refreshed your knowledge of the basic Scrum concepts

- understood how Scrum relates to conventional project management
- understood how Scrum relates to the (in)famous Waterfall method
- understood hoe Scrum relates to the Six Sigma project management
- acknowledged the power of a good ambiance in your Scrum team (and everything that encompasses)
- acknowledged that building a successful Scrum team is not about infusing them with the rules and regulations, but about infusing them with your own example.

Overall, I hope you have learned that Scrum is not the single project management method used out there, and that it may not even be the best in all circumstances. But when it *is* an option, Scrum is without doubt one of the very best paths to walk on.

More than that, I hope you have learned that Scrum is one of the most flexible project management methods, and that it is precisely why it can be fairly easily coordinated with other methods.

Congratulations on everything you have learned thus far. As simple as Scrum may be, I hope that this book has helped you with the understanding of the complexities behind Scrum and how even those are always narrowed down to a very specific, simple set of actions.

The power of Scrum extends well beyond the borders of project management and well into who you are as a human being, at a personal level. When you adhere to the values and principles of Scrum, you can live more organized, you can do more, and you can generally be more balanced in everything you do.

Scrum can help you be exactly who you want to be. It will help you be more honest with yourself. It will help you be more efficient in the way you tackle task after task. And it will help you be more self-confident in everything you do.

A new future is right in front of your eyes, all you have to do now is open the "Gates" of Scrum project management and embrace it.

Amazing things can happen when you place honesty and self-reliance over everything else and you will make no exception from this rule!

Bibliography

ALMA CLASSICS.(2018). *CANDIDE.*[S.l.].

Emmons, M. (2019).Key Statistics about Millennials in the Workplace | Dynamic Signal. Retrieved from https://dynamicsignal.com/2018/10/09/key-statistics-millennials-in-the-workplace/

Millennial Insights for the 2020 Labor Market. (2019). Retrieved from http://www.mrinetwork.com/articles/industry-articles/millennial-insights-for-the-2020-labor-market/

Publishing, H. (2019). Giving thanks can make you happier - Harvard Health. Retrieved from https://www.health.harvard.edu/healthbeat/giving-thanks-can-make-you-happier

THE IMPACT OF THE PHYSICAL WORK ENVIRONMENT ON ORGANIZATIONAL OUTCOMES: A STRUCTURED REVIEW OF THE LITERATURE. (2019). Retrieved from https://jfmer.org/doi/full/10.22361/jfmer/76637

Made in the USA
Las Vegas, NV
13 July 2021